Easy Bathroom Improvements

Julian Cassell
Peter Parham

TIME LIFE BOOKS

Alexandria, Virginia

TIME® LIFE BOOKS

TIME LIFE INC.
President and CEO Jim Nelson

TIME-LIFE TRADE PUBLISHING
Vice President and Publisher Neil Levin
Senior Director of Acquisitions and Editorial
Resources Jennifer Pearce
Director of New Product Development
   Carolyn Clark
Director of Trade Sales Dana Coleman
Director of Marketing Inger Forland
Director of New Product Development
   Teresa Graham
Director of Custom Publishing John Lalor
Director of Special Markets Robert Lombardi
Director of Design Kate L. McConnell
Project Manager Jennie Halfant

Originated in Singapore by Chroma Graphics.
Printed and bound in China by Excel Printing.
10 9 8 7 6 5 4 3 2 1

Front cover photography: **Tim Ridley** (top, centre
and bottom centre) **Camera Press** (bottom left)
Paul Ryan/ International Interiors (bottom right)
Back cover photography: **Tim Ridley**

TIME-LIFE is a trademark of Time Warner Inc., and
affiliated companies.

Library of Congress Cataloging-in-Publication Data
Cassell, Julian.
Easy bathroom improvements : the essential guide to
home decorating / Julian Cassell & Peter Parham.
   p. cm. — (Time-Life do-it-yourself factfile)
Includes index
ISBN: 0-7370-0309-X (spiral bound : alk. paper)
1. Bathrooms—Remodeling—Amateurs' manuals.
2. Interior decoration—Amateurs' manuals. 1. Parham,
Peter. II. Title. III. Series.

TH4816.3B37 C37 2000
643'.52—dc21   99-089110

Books produced by Time-Life Trade Publishing are
available at a special bulk discount for promotional
and premium use. Custom adaptations can also be
created to meet your specific marketing goals.
Call 1-800-323-5255.

Marshall Editions
Project Editor Felicity Jackson

Designed by Martin Lovelock & John Round

Photographer Tim Ridley

Illustrations Chris Forsey

Project Manager Nicholas Barnard

Managing Art Editor Patrick Carpenter

Managing Editor Antonia Cunningham

Editorial Director Ellen Dupont

Art Director Dave Goodman

Editorial Coordinator Ros Highstead

Production Anna Pauletti

Note

Every effort has been taken to ensure that all information in this book is correct and compatible with
national standards generally accepted at the time of publication. This book is not intended to replace
manufacturer's instructions in the use of their tools and materials—always follow their safety guidelines.
The author and publisher disclaim any liability, loss, injury or damage incurred as a consequence, directly
or indirectly, of the use and application of the contents of this book.

CONTENTS

INTRODUCTION

The bathroom is the one area of the home that provides a great opportunity to experiment with a large number of finishes—you can indulge yourself creating a look that satisfies all your needs and aspirations. A bathroom makeover can range from changing the faucet to total renovation and redecoration—both approaches, carried out properly, can be equally successful in producing a finish you can be proud of.

Because the bathroom is one of the most used rooms in the house, most of us like to create a comfortable and homely atmosphere that fits in with the rest of the household decoration. The main thing to remember is that the bathroom decoration must be practical and able to withstand the rigors of everyday use, as well as attractive and stylish. All the instructions for decorative finishes in this book keep these facts in mind, showing you how to deal with the main bathroom drawback—moist air and the problems it can cause. This book also explains how standard decorating techniques can be adjusted to create more durable, water-repellent finishes.

DESIGNING FOR THE SPACE

Whether you are deciding on the color scheme or designing storage facilities, always take the size of the room into account—bathrooms are often small rooms. From a purely decorative angle, it is easier to choose colors for a small room since swatches of paint on the walls can give a very good impression of the effect that color will have, whereas a swatch in a larger room with vast expanses of wall tends to get overshadowed. This also applies to samples of fabric, wallpaper, tiles, and floorcoverings. Make good use of samples provided by retailers before making any final decisions, and always look at the samples in the bathroom itself, so that the different colors, textures, and finishes can be seen in the actual surroundings they will be used in.

CLEVER STORAGE

Since bathrooms tend to be one of
the smaller rooms in the house, it is
essential that you utilize all available
space Making the best use of space
requires imaginative, well-designed
storage systems. The secret is to try
and provide functional areas that
also have lots of decorative appeal
and add to the look of the room as a
whole. Chapter 1 is full of creative
ideas for all those essential bathroom
items—places to store them or just
display them, tailored and finished to
your specific needs.

BATHROOM DECORATING

To a certain extent, the systems and
techniques used for decorating
bathrooms differ very little from
those methods used for other rooms
in the home, but there are extra
considerations. Chapter 2 provides
excellent, foolproof instruction on
decorating technique as a whole and
also discusses variations and different
ideas that are particularly suited to a
bathroom rather than other areas of
the home.

DEALING WITH FLOORS

Floor space is limited in most bathrooms so it is
important to choose the correct floorcovering,
paying particular attention to its practical qualities
as well as its decorative appeal. Chapter 3 explains
all the suitable options for bathroom floors, with
step-by-step directions on how to create the look
you require and the most appropriate techniques
for achieving it.

FIXTURE DETAILS

The accessories that turn a bathroom into a practical and functional room include things like the lighting, blinds, and mirrors. These are just a few of the examples found in Chapter 4, all of which combine to provide the finishing touches to a bathroom makeover. Take time to consider the mood you want to create, and the style requirements this will involve, before you choose your accessories since this will help you achieve the kind of bathroom you want.

PLUMBING AWARENESS

It is worthwhile for homeowners to be aware of how their plumbing system works, and where any potential problems may occur, because not all areas of plumbing need to be left to the professionals. Chapter 5 shows you how to carry out some of the simpler plumbing jobs, which can enable you to make changes in bathroom systems for both practical and decorative reasons. Understanding how your bathroom plumbing functions helps you to decide whether you need to call in a professional plumber when you are doing a complete or partial bathroom makeover.

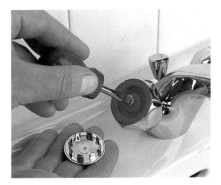

MAKING CHANGES

Changing the look of your bathroom can be an ongoing process—you may jump forward in large leaps, or progress slowly with small, well-thought-out improvements that gradually build up to a completely different atmosphere and finish. Chapter 6 provides ideas for this sort of gradual progression plus lots of ideas for those final touches, the last little details needed to complete the bathroom makeover.

ENJOYING A MAKEOVER

Decorating is a very rewarding pastime, producing a definite result that can be enjoyed every day. Add to this the other activities associated with a bathroom makeover and you have a complete extra dimension—bathroom makeovers should never be considered a laborious task, as the pleasure derived from the finished product is well worth all the effort. Always remember to spend as much time planning a makeover as actually carrying it out; having a set of guidelines and an order of work helps to direct you through the various processes in the correct sequence to complete the job satisfactorily. This book is the essential guide for all amateur home decorators, whatever the level of aptitude, providing plenty of ideas and instruction to help you to produce designs and finishes for your home, to enjoy now and in the years to come.

GENERAL TOOLS

A basic household toolbox is essential for carrying out bathroom makeovers, as there are some tools you will need time and time again during the process. Not all the tools shown here will be required at once, so it is important to prioritize and build up a larger toolbox over the years, until you are capable of dealing with every eventuality.

Hot-air gun

Chisels

Electrical tape

Adjustable wrench

Tape measure

Workbench

Brick chisel

Sander

Profile gauge

Staple gun

Cordless drill/driver

Short level

Dust mask

Panel saw

Hacksaw

Jigsaw

Hammer

Plastering float

Stepladder

Miter block

Straight-blade screwdrivers

Cross-head screwdrivers

Plier wrench

DECORATING TOOLS

I t is important to have a good selection of tools available to carry out the required decorations in the bathroom. Choose the items carefully, making sure that they are good value for money and capable of producing the best finish. More expensive equipment tends to be the best quality, producing excellent results and lasting long enough to be used for other decorating projects.

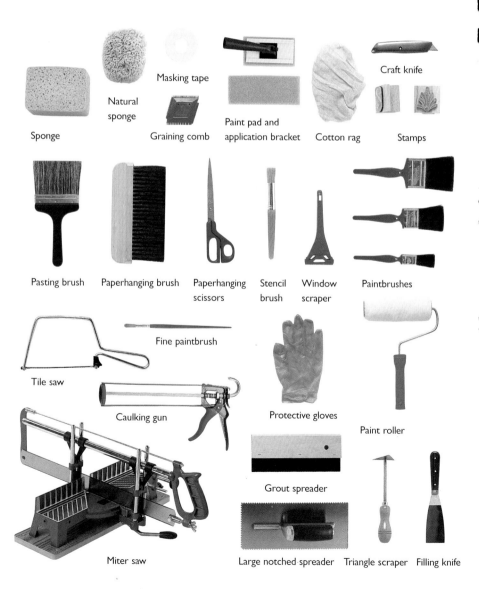

Masking tape

Natural sponge

Sponge

Graining comb

Paint pad and application bracket

Cotton rag

Craft knife

Stamps

Pasting brush

Paperhanging brush

Paperhanging scissors

Stencil brush

Window scraper

Paintbrushes

Fine paintbrush

Tile saw

Caulking gun

Protective gloves

Paint roller

Grout spreader

Miter saw

Large notched spreader

Triangle scraper

Filling knife

CLEVER STORAGE

Generally bathrooms are one of the smaller rooms in the home, with limited floor space which can restrict freedom of movement. Despite its size, however, the bathroom is still very busy and needs plenty of storage and display space for towels, toiletries, and decorative accessories. The secret of clever storage in bathrooms is to create as much space as possible through the design of the storage areas, keeping them attractive as well so that they become decorative items rather than functional eyesores. Cunning shelf design, using areas otherwise considered as wasted space, and well-thought-out hanging systems, all add to the appeal of the room.

DECIDING ON STORAGE AREAS

There are all sorts of factors to consider when choosing bathroom storage. You have to decide how practical these areas need to be and balance it with their decorative appeal. House size as a whole is important—in many cases the linen closet and storage space for toiletries must be included in the bathroom. Where these can be built in other parts of the house, storage in the bathroom becomes less vital, and decorative shelving and display areas can be more important.

Combining storage and style: open shelving allows for both storage and display; it is a very practical way of housing items vital to bathroom activities and combines this function with an ordered look, keeping things close at hand and easy to find.

Practical storage: well-designed shelving is an excellent space-saving facility, making use of otherwise wasted areas of the bathroom, and accommodating lots of items in a relatively small space.

The built-in approach: a neat, compact finish is easy to achieve if you have a number of built-in cabinets. These maximize storage while minimizing space wastage. Professional help may be required to produce a perfect custom-made finish, although many retailers do sell "flat-packed" cabinet and shelving systems that are relatively simple to assemble and install.

Maintaining ventilation: bathrooms are prone to high levels of moisture in the air, so it is essential to keep them well ventilated. This is an important consideration with the storage facilities—cabinet doors that allow air to circulate are very helpful, especially in smaller bathrooms.

STORAGE IDEAS

- Displaying and concealing: it is always a good idea to have some storage areas that can be used to show off attractive items, but it is equally important to have unobtrusive cabinets and shelving for storing items that do not necessarily warrant open viewing.
- Child-proofing: medicines are often kept in bathroom cabinets and these

cabinets should be positioned out of the reach of children and, if possible, have a lock on them.
- Dual purpose: combining functions is the secret of clever storage; for example, a wall cabinet containing a mirror or a shelf with hooks on the underside are prime examples of maximizing space by having one item fulfill two jobs.

USING CORNERS

C orners are often wasted areas of a room, especially in bathrooms, where sinks and other fixtures prevent larger pieces of furniture from being positioned there. Corner storage systems tend to require securing into the walls, rather than having a fixed base. All kinds of corner units can be bought from retailers, but, using a few simple ideas, you can create clever designs of your own, such as tile shelving.

TILE SHELVING

Tiles are often used to form shelved areas in bathrooms, but this is normally confined to bathtub ledges or window sills. A more innovative use is to just use the tiles themselves, as single shelves in their own right. Large floor tiles are ideal for this purpose and can be used to create novel corner shelving.

1 Mark a diagonal line from corner to corner across a floor tile, using a piece of batten for a straight edge. Using a tile cutter, cut two identical triangular shapes.

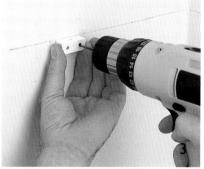

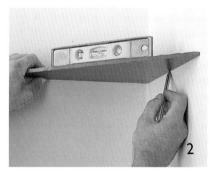

2 Hold the tile, wrong side down, at the approximate required level in the corner and adjust its position until it is level. Make a pencil mark on the wall along the underside of the tile.

3 Hold a jointing block just below the pencil line and drill two pilot holes. Depending on the wall, you may need wall anchors in order to provide a firm fixing hole for the screws.

4 Screw in the jointing block, then position another close to it. Position two more blocks on the adjacent wall.

5 Position a tile on the blocks and apply a gloss or mat varnish to the cut edge of the tile, depending on the finish required. The shelves can be left so that they can be easily removed. Alternatively, to make the shelf more secure, some adhesive can be applied to the top of each jointing block before the tile is positioned.

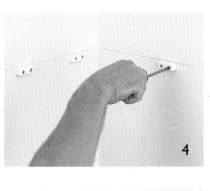

4

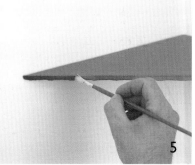

5

ADDING MORE SHELVES
Add more shelves to the corner as required. Since the jointing blocks are small enough to hide how the tiles are attached, they do not detract from the look of this "suspended" tile shelving.

PRACTICAL CORNER STORAGE

C orner spaces are ideal for use as practical storage areas. These will add to the decoration of the room while making maximum use of the space. They also give you the opportunity to test your skills by building across the corner and creating open storage systems. Precise measurements and accurate cutting are essential if you want to produce excellent results.

MAKING A TOWEL STACK

Bathrooms are always full of towels and these are often hidden away in closets. Displaying them gives you the chance to make an otherwise dull storage system far more attractive, and keeping them in the open means they are well ventilated and within easy reach.

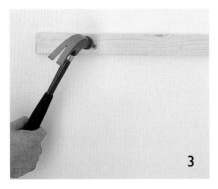

1 Measure out 18 in (45 cm) from the corner and draw a level line from this point back to the corner.

2 Cut an 18-in (45-cm) length of 2-by-½-in (5-by-1-cm) batten, mitering one end.

3 Attach the batten above the pencil line, using two masonry nails, with the mitered end pointing away from the corner. Attach a corresponding batten, 17½ in (44 cm) in length, on the adjacent wall. Measure the distance between the end point of the miter on each wall, and cut another length of batten to this size, mitering the cuts so that the ends of the batten will fit snugly against the wall.

4 Nail the batten in place with brads. Continue to attach more battens along the top of the frame, measuring ¾ in (2 cm) along the wall toward the corner for each new length of wood.

5 Cut a 12-in (30-cm) length of batten and nail it vertically, set back slightly from the corner of the first horizontal batten. Continue to add three more battens at equal distances to the corner. Repeat these vertical lengths on the adjacent wall.

6 Repeat Steps 1–4 to produce another horizontal slatted platform below the vertical battens. Finish the wood with varnish or color rub with a latex paint, as shown here. Leave the paint to dry then seal the wood with a coat of varnish. Allow it to dry before use.

COLORFUL AND ELEGANT
A towel stack creates a colorful and elegant piece of practical shelving.

SIMPLE SHELVES

S omething simple is often the most effective kind of shelving. There is no specific design for a simple shelf, except that it should be as uncomplicated as possible and provide enough support for the objects it will hold. Make sure that the finished shelf is level on the wall and choose a finish that will complement the decorative style of the room.

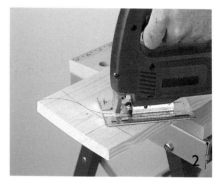

1 On a length of 5-by-1-in (12.5-by-2.5-cm) softwood, measure 2½ in (6 cm) in from each corner. Draw lines at right angles to these marks to make a cross, then use a paint can to draw three curves in a bracket shape.

2 Use a jigsaw to cut along the curved pencil guideline. Follow the manufacturer's safety instructions when using a jigsaw, and never stand in front of the blade. Repeat Steps 1 and 2 to make a second bracket.

3 Cut another length of 5-by-1-in (12.5-by-2.5-cm) prepared softwood to the required length for your shelf. Hold a bracket 5 in (12.5 cm) in from the cut end, drawing a pencil guideline along the point where the bracket meets the shelf.

4 Hold the bracket securely on the guideline and drill a pilot hole through the bracket into the shelf.

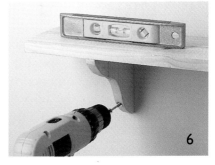

5 Drive a screw into the hole (see below), making sure that it bites firmly into the shelf, but does not go all the way through to what will be the shelf top. For extra strength, apply some wood glue to the bracket before positioning it on the guideline. Attach the other bracket to the shelf in the same way.

6 Drill two more holes in the brackets for wall attachment. Position the shelf using a level, then screw through the brackets into the wall, using wall anchors, if necessary. For added strength, drill and fix two screws at a 45-degree angle through the top of the shelf (at the back), through the brackets, and into the wall. Fill all screw holes. Round the corners of the shelf with sandpaper.

DECORATIVE
STORAGE SYSTEM
Once decorated, a simple shelf provides an attractive decorative storage system for ornaments or items in everyday use.

FIXING THE SCREWS

Use a countersink drill bit to open up the entrance to the drilled hole on the bracket, so that the screw will fit below the wood surface.

WALL-SUSPENDED SHELVES

Allowing the majority of the weight of a shelf to be supported from above, rather than below, produces an interesting effect quite different from the more traditional shelves. Combining wood with rope, and using large obvious wall fixings, adds to the sturdy, uncomplicated design of a wall-suspended shelf. The rustic appeal of this kind of design lends itself to a very natural looking finish, such as waxing, a distressed paint effect, or a simple color rub.

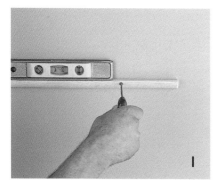

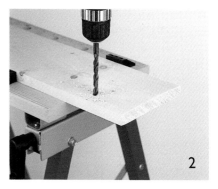

1 Cut a piece of ¾-in (2-cm) quadrant to the same length as your shelf (5-by-1-in/12.5-by-2.5-cm planed softwood is ideal for the shelf), here cut to 2 ft (60 cm). Screw the quadrant into the wall at the required shelf height using a short level to make sure that it is level. Drill pilot holes and insert wall anchors, if necessary, to ensure a good fixing.

2 Measure 1 in (2.5 cm) in from the edge of the shelf, and 3 in (7.5 cm) from its end, and make a pencil mark. Drill a hole at this mark, using a bit of a similar size to the rope being used to support the shelf—a diameter of ¼ in (7.5 mm) is ideal. Make another hole in the corresponding position at the other end of the shelf.

3 Cut two lengths of rope to about 18 in (45 cm) long. Thread one piece through each hole in the shelf and tie each piece with a knot on the underside, as shown.

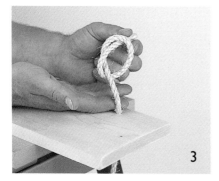

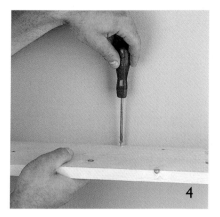

4 Position the shelf above the quadrant on the wall, making sure that the shelf edge is tight up against the wall/quadrant junction. Screw in three wood screws at equal distances along the back edge of the shelf, screwing through the shelf and into the quadrant below.

5 In a vertical line from the drilled rope holes, screw two large "eye" brackets into the wall about 10 in (25 cm) above the shelf. If necessary, drill a pilot hole before using a screwdriver as a lever to screw the "eye" into the wall. Once both "eyes" are in position, thread the two loose ends of the rope through their corresponding "eye," and tie them so that the rope is taut.

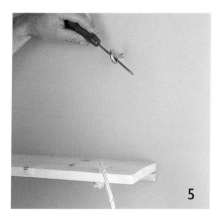

NATURAL LOOK
This shelf has been finished with a white liming, or pickling, wax to protect and decorate the wood, while maintaining its natural look.

CEILING-SUSPENDED SHELVES

S helving can be designed to hang from the ceiling, rather than using the wall as the main weight support. For this kind of shelving, it is essential to find a strong fixing point—a solid wooden joist—as the entire weight of the hanging shelf is taken by this one point. However, once this obstacle is overcome, suspended ceiling shelving creates an excellent effect, giving you secure shelving without any cumbersome supports. Three shelves are ideal for creating a balanced looking shelving system.

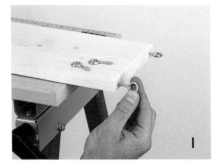

1 Cut three 18-in (45-cm) lengths from 5-by-1-in (12.5-by-2.5-cm) planed softwood. At one end of each length, screw in two small "eyes," ½ in (12 mm) from the edge. Screw in two "eyes" at the other end of each shelf in the corresponding position.

2 Using wire cutters, cut four pieces of chain each measuring 3 feet (90 cm) in length.

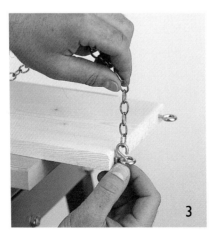

3 Attach the bottom link of one chain to each of the four "eyes" on one of the shelves, using chain hooks. Measure 20 cm (8 in) up each chain and position another shelf, and finally measure the same distance again and position the final shelf. On the chain shown here, 20 cm (8 in) is the same as 20 links of the chain, which is an easy way of measuring between "eyes."

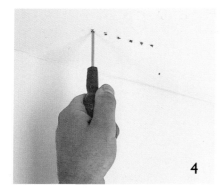

4

5

4 To find a firm fixing point in the ceiling, make a number of holes with an old screwdriver or bradawl until you find a solid wooden joist. Try and find a fixing position no more than 3 in (7.5 cm) away from the wall, so that the shelf will gain some small support from the wall to prevent it from spinning around.

5 Screw a large hook into the fixing hole. Use a screwdriver as leverage to make sure that the hook is solidly screwed into place. Fill in the other holes. Take the four loose ends of chain and position the final link of each four over the hook, adjusting the chains into the correct position, if necessary.

SUSPENDING SHELVES
Once in place, all the effort of suspending shelving is well worthwhile. A simple colored stain is the ideal way of finishing the shelves to create a stunning suspended shelving system.

RACKS AND RAILS

S helves and traditional towel rails can be adapted to give them a more innovative appearance, while still maintaining their use as storage facilities. Playing with ideas can be great fun, allowing for freedom of expression and the chance to try something new.

TOOTHBRUSH-MUG RACK

The idea of a toothbrush-mug rack is by no means new, but some simple design changes, such as keeping the shelf very angular, and decorating it with something like metallic paint, can give it an ultramodern look. For the design below, the toothbrush mug must have a larger rim than the base.

1   Cut a length of 5-by-1-in (12.5-by-2.5-cm) planed softwood to the required length, allowing for two triangular brackets to be cut from this length. Hold a toothbrush mug central to the shelf, but to one side of its width, and pencil a guideline.

2   Use a jigsaw to cut out both brackets. Drill a hole at the edge of the circular guideline to accommodate the jigsaw blade, and cut out the central area. Attach the brackets and the shelf to the wall.

SIMPLISTIC
This simplistic rack can be painted to match any color scheme and will look perfectly at home in any modern bathroom.

TOWEL RAILS

A novel towel rail can be produced from simple copper pipes of the type used for home plumbing. By combining straight lengths of pipe with right-angled joints and T-shaped connectors, it is possible to create all sorts of shapes and designs. Use a proprietary adhesive capable of securing two metal surfaces to stick the joints together.

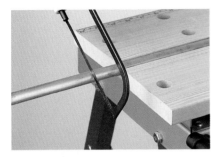

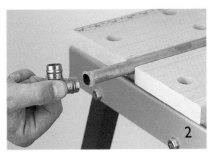

1 Decide on the dimensions of the towel rail you require, then cut lengths of pipe to size. Pipe cutters can be used, but a sharp hacksaw will do the job just as efficiently.

2 Glue elbow joints and T connectors to the pipe lengths, making sure that there is a strong bond. Wipe off any excess adhesive before it dries.

3 Drill holes through the T connectors that back onto the wall surface. Fix them in place on the wall before the rest of the framework is built up to give the finished rail no visible fixing points. Before using, coat the rail with a good quality varnish to prevent damp towels from corroding the copper, and the towels themselves from becoming stained.

SLOPING FRAMEWORK
On this design, the two lower sets of the three pipes at the side of the framework become increasingly shorter as they go down the rack. When towels are hung on each level, they miss the towel below, which allows them to dry faster.

BATHTUB HATCHES

There are sometimes areas at the foot or head of an inset bathtub that are underused and waste their space-saving capabilities. Instead of totally boxing in these areas, you can insert a door in the boxing and use the space as storage cabinets. Bathtub hatches need to be inserted according to the specific design of your bathtub (see opposite); however, there are certain points that must be considered before building any such storage system.

HINGING HATCHES

It is essential that hatch doors fit precisely and that their hinging mechanism ensures that the door sits flush. Use the aptly named "flush" hinges—these hinges are relatively easy to attach and run all the way along the hinged edge of the hatch, making a very precise finish to the door edge.

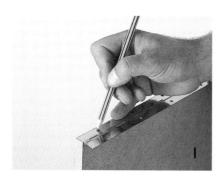

1 Cut the bathtub hatch to the right size and clamp it vertically onto a workbench. Cut the flush hinge to length, using a hacksaw, and hold the hinge along the appropriate edge of the hatch, marking the screw positions with a pencil.

2 Remove the hinge and drill pilot holes at the pencil marks on the hatch.

3 Hold the hinge along the edge, and fix it in place with the appropriate size screws. Holding the hinged hatch in place, mark the position for the corresponding hinge holes, drill the pilot holes, and screw it in position.

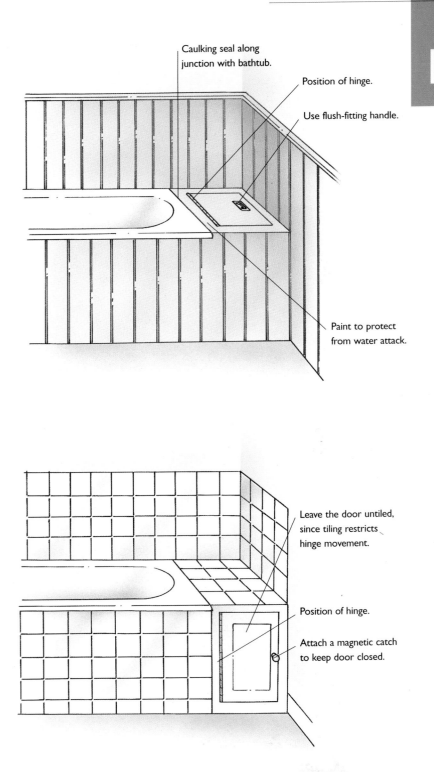

Caulking seal along junction with bathtub.

Position of hinge.

Use flush-fitting handle.

Paint to protect from water attack.

Leave the door untiled, since tiling restricts hinge movement.

Position of hinge.

Attach a magnetic catch to keep door closed.

HOOKS AND PEGS

Hooks and pegs are ideal for hanging towels, bathrobes, and general bathroom odds and ends. Hooks are usually positioned on the back of doors, or out of the way in corners and alcoves. However, with some smooth wooden doweling and planed softwood you can make a wooden peg rack attractive enough to take pride of place in your bathroom.

1 Cut a 2-ft (60-cm) length of 5-by-1-in (12.5-by-2.5-cm) board. Divide the board into five equal sections 4¾ in (12 cm) wide, marking each one with a pencil guideline. Bisect the pencil lines with another guideline across the length of the board.

2 Using a drill bit that corresponds to the size of dowel you are using, drill into the board at the pencil line cross sections. Hold the drill at a slight angle and keep it consistent for all four holes. Try not to allow the bit to go all the way through the plank.

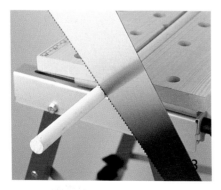

3 Using a saw, cut four lengths of wooden dowel, each measuring 6 in (15 cm) long.

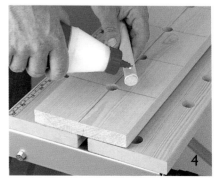

4 Apply a generous amount of wood glue to one end of each wooden dowel.

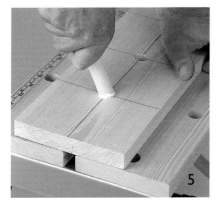

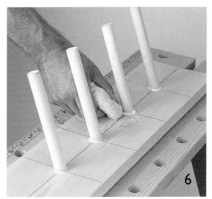

5 Carefully insert one dowel into each of the drilled holes in the plank of wood.

6 Remove any excess glue with a rag before it dries. Allow the peg rack to dry completely before painting it.

BATHROOM ESSENTIALS

Once painted and attached to the wall, this peg rack makes an attractive storage system that is ideal for hanging all manner of bathroom essentials.

SINK STORAGE

T he area around sinks is often wasted as far as storage space is concerned. Creating a vanity unit is one option for utilizing this area. A more simplistic approach is to make a curtain divide. This can easily be blended in with other soft furnishings in the room, and the decoration as a whole. All that is required is some self-adhesive hook-and-loop tape and either one or two curtains to fit the required area.

1 Unroll a section of hook-and-loop tape and stick one side of it around the edge of the sink, about 2 in (5 cm) from the rim of the sink. Although the sink profile makes it difficult to keep the tape smooth and level, try to avoid creases and keep it as parallel to the rim as possible. Any small undulations will be covered by the curtain.

2 Attach the other side of the hook-and-loop tape to the back of the curtain or curtains, and carefully press until the curtain adheres to the tape. This method of attachment means it is very easy to remove the curtain for cleaning.

VANITY UNIT
A vanity unit is a more complicated form of sink storage, which requires a great deal more planning and considerable carpentry skills. However, the end product looks extremely attractive while creating a practical, hidden storage system.

DECORATING WALLS

The decoration of a bathroom usually plays the most important part in giving the room its overall look, and colors and finishes need to be carefully considered. General decorating ideas apply in the usual way, but some practical requirements must be taken into consideration. Bathroom activities make tiles ideal for some of the wall surfaces, while paper and paint should be chosen with due regard for their hardwearing properties. This chapter explains how surfaces should be prepared and how decorating materials are applied to make them suitable for bathroom use.

CHOOSING A STYLE

A bathroom is often dominated by one particular type of decorating material, which may be tiles, wallpaper, or paint. If there is a strong theme, other features in the room need to complement this. The secret of a pleasing decorative look is to get the balance right between the main theme and the smaller details, and produce a well-coordinated finished product.

2

Papering: wallpapering is the easiest way to create an instant pattern, as well as provide texture and warmth in what can be a small and cramped room. Vinyl papers are best in bathrooms as they are durable and can be wiped easily. It is doubly important in a bathroom to make sure that the paper is well stuck down, especially around the edges and along seams.

Painting the walls: the quickest way to change the look of a bathroom is to paint the walls. The woodwork can then be painted to match the walls—with the vast range of colors available, it is very easy to find just the color you want. Shades of blue always work well since they provide a clean and fresh feel that balances well with the bathroom environment.

Dominating with tiles: tiles are always a very practical decorative material to use in a bathroom—extremely easy to keep clean and very durable. A tiled theme can produce an impressive and highly decorative finish, which will last for years. As with the color blue, shades of green tend to produce a refreshing feel that is ideal for a larger bathroom.

2

IDEAS FOR A SCHEME

- Colors: in smaller rooms, lighter colors provide a greater feeling of space; darker shades can be used to highlight detailed areas, such as shelves and window frames.
- Renovating or redecorating: if you are having an entirely new bathroom, it is worth taking a little extra time to ensure that the decoration harmonizes with the fixtures—it will be dependent on the color of these fixtures. Any wall color will complement new white fixtures, but if you choose strong colors for bathtubs and sinks, coordinating the scheme will be more difficult and future redecoration choices more limited.
- Attention to detail: bathrooms tend to be small, which means that all surfaces are close to the eye and

prone to close scrutiny. Also, the very fact that people lounge in the bathtub gives plenty of opportunity for inspecting the decoration, and means that particular attention must be paid to all details in the room. It makes surface preparation that much more important, and the overall finishing requires extra care in order to produce the best possible result.
- Comfort: when choosing colors or textures, remember that the bathroom is an area where you want to be able to relax. An awareness of the effects of color is important. Strong colors can be used, but bear in mind that they may not be restful. It really depends on your own personal preference and what sort of atmosphere and feel you want the decoration to create.

WHAT TO USE WHERE

S ome bathrooms are more suited to particular materials than others, and, more importantly, specific areas in the room are better suited to one finish than another. You need to understand the particular properties of the various materials in order to use them in the right place and to the best effect.

2

TILES

Tiles are ideal for nearly all bathroom surfaces, but it is worth considering their size and shape, as well as the color and finish, to determine what is going to be most suitable for your requirements.

TILES IN THE BATHROOM

- Finish: it is best to use glazed rather than unglazed tiles, since the former are much easier to keep clean and therefore more durable.
- Size: although large tiles cover areas more quickly, they will show up any undulations or defects in wall surfaces much more readily. Also, a particularly small room is not ideal for large tiles since a lot of intricate cuts are required, accuracy becomes more tricky, and sticking large tiles into awkward areas can be very difficult.
- Showers and bathtubs: tiles are one of the most commonly used decorating materials around bathtubs and in showers because of their water-repellent properties. However, these properties only apply if grouting and sealing are carried out correctly—tiling is not complete until the surface is totally waterproof.
- Using the range: tiles are available in all manner of sizes, shapes, and colors, including border tiles, mosaic tesserae tiles, and tiled scenes. Surfaces need not be bland or repetitive; you can be as extravagant as you like. Combining different colors, patterns, and texture in your own individual style can be very rewarding.

PAINT

Paint is the most readily available of all decorating materials and is very easy to use. However, it is important to use the right paint in the right place, especially where bathrooms are concerned.

PAINT IN THE BATHROOM

- Hardwearing: the most hardwearing paints used to be oil- or solvent-based, but improved-formula, water-based equivalents are now nearly, if not totally, as good as their oil-based counterparts. Many manufacturers produce specific bathroom or moisture-resistant paints, which are ideal for bathroom surfaces. Otherwise, paints that contain vinyl can be wiped easily and are ideal for bathroom use.
- Drying times: the other advantage of water-based paints is that they dry quickly, allowing for more than one coat to be applied in a day. Because the bathroom is such a busy area, this means that the job can be completed quickly with little household upheaval.
- Around bathtubs and backsplashes: although this is normally the domain of tiles, these areas can be painted to good effect. Tongue-and-groove paneling looks particularly impressive around bathtubs (see page 103). However, because of the constant water splashes, it is advisable to use a waterproof paint.
- Make sure that you follow the manufacturer's safety advice for ventilation during painting.

2

WALLPAPER IN THE BATHROOM

- Hardwearing: use vinyl papers or, alternatively, varnish standard wallpapers after they have been applied.
- Avoiding damp: it is essential to keep paper away from areas prone to water splashes or excess moisture, such as backsplashes or the areas directly around bathtubs. When first applied, wallpaper looks great, but in no time at all, the surface will deteriorate if it gets damp, whether it is vinyl-coated or protected with varnish.
- Extra adhesive: overlap adhesive can be used along the edges of all lengths of paper to ensure a better seal and make the paper less likely to lift.

WALLPAPER

There is no problem with using wallpaper in bathrooms as long as you follow the guidelines (see left) and use the correct type of paper.

PAINTING TECHNIQUES

A sound painting technique is the key to good finishing. It is important to use all decorating tools in the manner for which they were designed. Some tools can be used in a number of places, others are designed for specific areas. Before any painting can begin, though, surfaces must be prepared and a working sequence planned.

COVERING UP

Surfaces that are not going to be painted must be covered up since paint spray is difficult to remove, and serious spillages can result in ruined floorcoverings. General-purpose drop cloths are ideal for most surfaces, but tiles and fixtures need extra care.

Masking tiles: paint-roller spray manages to find the smallest of areas to mark, such as the edges of tiles. Stick some masking tape along the top edge of tiles to protect them before you start painting.

Masking fixtures: bathroom fixtures are particularly awkward shapes to cover. Lightweight plastic drop cloths are the best thing to use. Secure them with masking tape to keep them in place while painting is in progress.

PREPARING SURFACES

Thorough surface preparation is required before any decorating can take place—this is the process that makes the difference between an average finish and an excellent one.

- Wall surfaces: strip old wallpaper, fill holes, and sand to a smooth finish. On particularly dusty surfaces, apply a coat of general-purpose builder's sealant to seal the walls before decorating.

- Wood: fill and sand as required.
- Washing down: wash down all the surfaces with a mild detergent, rinse and let dry before painting.
- Primers: on bare wood, use a good quality primer before applying the undercoat, and top coats. On unpainted plaster, size the surface for further coats by diluting the first coat of water-based paint by one part water to 10 parts paint.

CHOOSING A TECHNIQUE

There are advantages and disadvantages with all the different methods of painting (see below). Choose the technique that suits you best and is the most appropriate for the conditions in your bathroom.

2

BRUSHES	The most multipurpose of all painting tools. Ideal for all areas because of the different sizes available. Pure bristle brushes are still the best quality, although some synthetic-fiber brushes are excellent for water-based paints.
ROLLERS	Make fast work of large open areas, but a brush will still be required to cut in around wall and ceiling edges. Choose the coarseness of the roller sleeve according to the finish required and the condition of the walls. Mohair rollers produce an exceptionally smooth finish.
PAINT PADS	Have the covering capability of rollers, are easy to use and economic on paint usage. Small pads can be used around edges although a brush is often a better option.
PAINT SPRAYERS	Ideal for covering large areas quickly, but you need to mask off all the places that must be kept free of paint. Because of the multisurfaced nature of bathrooms and the lack of space, they are not ideally suited to this area of the home. Also, breathing apparatus is normally required when using paint sprayers.

CAUTION

When using paint, always make sure that the area is well ventilated—this is particularly important in a small bathroom. Leave windows and doors open to ensure a good through-draft of air. Bathrooms often have slippery surfaces, so be careful since drop cloths can slip on floors. Keep children and pets well out of the way while painting is in progress.

TILING TECHNIQUES

I t is almost certain that at some stage you will need to apply tiles to a bathroom wall. Understanding the basics of tiling is essential if you want to achieve a good finish: the secret is sound preparation, starting at the correct point, and ensuring the tiles are applied securely.

PREPARING SURFACES

2

Different surfaces need different preparation before tiles can be applied. Tile application will be more difficult and less effective if the surface is not properly prepared.

NEW PLASTER	Always seal new plaster with a coat of general-purpose builder's sealant. This stops the adhesive drying out too quickly when it is applied to the wall—which can turn tiling into a rushed job.
OLD PLASTER	As long as old plaster is sound, tiles can be applied directly to it. Fill any large holes with one-coat plaster; smaller areas can be filled with an all-purpose filler.
DRY-LINED	Dry-lined walls must be sealed with a coat of general-purpose builder's sealant in the same way as new plaster to prevent adhesive drying out too quickly.
OLD TILES	As long as old tiles are securely attached to the wall, there is no reason why new tiles may not be applied directly over the top of them. Make sure that the old tiles are cleaned and sanded to give their surface a key for accepting adhesive. Any loose tiles should be removed and their spaces filled with patch plaster. However, if the tiled surface has a number of loose or broken tiles, it is best to start afresh by removing all the tiles with a cold chisel and hammer. Wear goggles to protect your eyes from flying debris when carrying out this process.
WALLPAPER	Wallpaper must be removed from walls before tiling—use a steam stripper to speed up the process. Once all the paper is removed, fill holes, as necessary, then sand and, finally, seal the surface with a general-purpose sealant.

ORDER OF WORK

Bathroom layouts vary, but there are certain guidelines that apply to nearly all rooms in order to achieve the best tiling results.

Follow the order of work so that Area 1 is finished before Area 2, and so on. Within each area, start at the bottom and work upward.

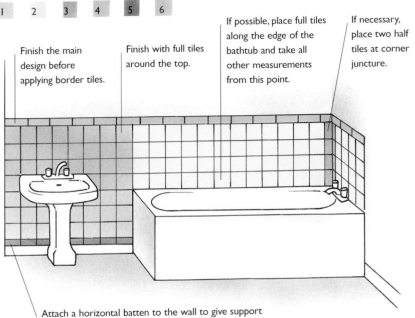

1 2 3 4 5 6

Finish the main design before applying border tiles.

Finish with full tiles around the top.

If possible, place full tiles along the edge of the bathtub and take all other measurements from this point.

If necessary, place two half tiles at corner juncture.

2

Attach a horizontal batten to the wall to give support for Area 1 to be tiled. Remove the batten once the tile adhesive has set, in order to tile Area 5.

TECHNIQUE GUIDE

- Use wooden battens nailed level into walls as starting supports for the first rows of tiles. It is rare that the top of baseboards are precisely level, and centralizing tile layouts often means that half tiles are required at the bottom of walls and the batten supports the first rows.
- Keep tile surfaces as flush as possible; reduce the tile adhesive on the back of any tiles that stick

out from the wall, and add tile adhesive to those that appear to have sunk.
- Keep some clean water and a sponge handy at all times so that the excess tile adhesive can be cleaned off tile surfaces before it has a chance to set.
- Buy a good-quality tile cutter to make straight cuts, and a tile saw for dealing with curves and cutting holes for pipes.

HALF-TILING A BATHROOM

H alf-tiling a room offers the opportunity to combine tiled finishes with paper and/or paint to create a blend of different surfaces. Such a project involves all the basic tiling techniques and demonstrates the approach and work sequence necessary for most tiling jobs.

1 Nail a horizontal supporting batten above the baseboard, making sure it is level. The gap left between this first row of tiles and the baseboard should be the size of half a tile. Avoid leaving a gap that will require small slithers since these are difficult to cut. Nail a vertical batten close to the corner to make a firm edge to butt the tiles against. Apply tile adhesive to an area of about one square yard (meter) and stick the tiles to the wall. Use tile spacers to maintain even gaps between the tiles.

3 Apply tile adhesive to the back of the cut tiles and position them along the corner junction. Make sure that the cut edge of each tile is positioned next to the corner, and use spacers to maintain even gaps between the tiles.

2 When the main wall surface has been tiled, remove the vertical batten and fill in along the corner junction with cut tiles. Mark the cut required on each tile with a fiber-tip pen, then use a tile cutter to score a line along the surface of the tile at the marked position. Once scored, move the tile up to between the bracket above the cutting wheel and below the sliding rails, positioning the scored line directly between the rails. Push down with even pressure to break the tile along the line.

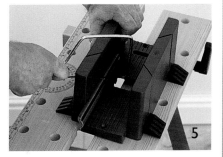

4 Once the walls are covered with the main body of tiles to the required level, border tiles can be applied around the top edge of the tiles. Apply a generous amount of adhesive to the back of border tiles with a scraper, then position them.

6 Position the mitered tile in the corner then continue with border tiles along the adjacent wall. Once the border is complete allow the tile adhesive to set before grouting. When the grout has dried, polish the entire tiled surface with a dry cotton rag.

5 Relief border tiles, as shown here, require mitered joints in the corners in order to produce the best possible finish. Make the appropriate measurement, place the tile in a miter block, then cut through it at the desired position with a tile saw.

2

BORDER TILE FRAME
Half-tiled rooms produce an attractive finish, with border tiles acting as the frame to the main body of tiles. A simple color combination produces a very restful atmosphere.

PAINTING TILES

T iles can be given an alternative finish by painting them. The finish of painted tiles will not be as durable as the ordinary glazed surface but, as long as the painted tiles are not under constant water attack, they have a good life expectancy.

PRIMING THE TILES

Changing the entire surface color of tiles requires thorough preparation to make sure that the paint adheres to the tiled surface. Before beginning, ensure that any gaps in the grout are filled and any broken tiles are replaced.

1 Clean the tiled surface with a mild detergent solution and then rinse with clean water. Allow the whole surface to dry.

2 Rub down the surface with abrasive siliconcarbide paper. This scratches the glazed surface of the tiles and provides a key for the paint. Once sanded, wipe down the area again with a damp sponge to remove any dusty residue. Allow the surface to dry.

3 Paint the entire tile surface with proprietary tile primer and leave it to dry. This paint is specially formulated to provide a sound base for the application of coats of finishing paint.

CREATING A DESIGN

Most types of paint can be used to produce the desired color or finish, as long as they are sealed with varnish after they have been applied. As an alternative to one solid color, any number of different tile patterns can be created—the checkerboard design below is one simple, yet effective example.

Painting a checkerboard: paint the entire primed surface with white latex paint then paint alternate tiles with black latex paint. Use a fine paintbrush to produce neat straight lines. Leave the paint to dry, then varnish the entire tiled surface to protect the finish.

2

USING CERAMICS

For the more adventurous decorator, small hand-painted designs can be applied to tiles with ceramic paint. Again, this paint finish should only be used in areas that are not under regular water attack.

1

2

1 Trace a design from a book using a pencil. Stick the image to a tile with masking tape, making sure that it is centrally positioned on the tile and the penciled side of the tracing paper is against the tile surface. Scribble over the outlines to transfer the pencil image onto the tile.

2 Remove the tracing paper, and carefully fill in the design, using ceramic paints. Allow the paint to dry, then varnish the entire tile surface to protect the design.

TRANSFERS AND STENCILS

Transfers and stencils are excellent decorations for transforming the look of tiles, especially when an old surface needs reviving, rather than totally replacing. Although transfers give a less hard-wearing surface than the standard glazed tiles, they are becoming more durable and are therefore perfectly acceptable to use on tiles.

2

APPLYING TRANSFERS

Transfers are fairly delicate, and they require a great deal of care when moving them from their backing paper onto the tile. Manufacturers' guidelines vary, but this method is typical of the procedure recommended for most types.

1 Clean the tile that is going to have the transfer applied to it with a mild detergent, then rinse with clean water. Leave it to dry.

2 Soak the transfer (on its backing paper) in warm water for about 20 seconds, then apply directly to the tile, as close to the required position as possible. The transfer should slide off the backing paper smoothly—the dampness of the area allows for final positioning of it before evaporation secures the image in place.

3 Using a dry rag, very carefully dab the surface of the transfer to remove any small air bubbles and excess moisture.

STENCILING TILES

Most paints can be used to stencil on tiles—it is the method of protecting the finish that is the secret of making sure that a stenciled image is long-lasting. Tiles can be primed first (see page 42), but it is not essential for such detailed painted areas. Make sure that the tiles are cleaned and allowed to dry thoroughly before applying the stencil.

I Stick the stencil securely in position on the tile surface using masking tape.

2 Apply paint with a stencil brush, using short dabbing motions and keeping the angle of the bristles as perpendicular as possible to the tiled surface. Remove the excess paint from the brush before applying it, otherwise the paint may seep under the edges of the stencil and distort the finished picture.

3 Remove the stencil carefully and leave the paint to dry. Meanwhile, wash the stencil and dry it thoroughly. Tape the stencil directly over the dried painted image on the tile, and apply some ceramic varnish, using the stencil brush. Make sure that all areas of the image are covered. Remove the stencil and allow the varnish to dry, producing a well-protected stencil image.

APPLYING WALLPAPER

T he method of paperhanging in a bathroom is the same as in any other room in the house, but there are special precautions you can take to make sure that the paper lasts as long as possible. Although vinyl papers are the best option for bathrooms, other papers can be used as long as a few extra precautions are taken (see box below).

BEFORE TILING

A complete bathroom makeover provides the opportunity to wallpaper before any tiles are applied. Although this is not the essential order of work, it does help to guarantee a long-lasting wallpaper finish.

1 Draw an accurate pencil guideline to show where the final row of tiles will be positioned on the wall. Apply the wallpaper so that the bottom edge comes approximately ½ in (12 mm) below the pencil line.

2 When the wallpapering is complete and the tiles are applied, the top row of tiles will cover this bottom edge of the paper and prevent it from lifting when the bathroom is damp and steamy.

STRENGTHENING THE PASTE

- Pastable papers: if using wallpapers that require pasting before application, make the paste mix slightly stronger than the manufacturer's recommendations for that type of paper. This makes a firmer bond with the wall and extends the life of the wallpaper.
- Prepasted wallpapers: the soaking and application process is normally enough to secure these wallpapers on walls in most rooms; however, for a bathroom it may be worth "double pasting" them. Although prepasted paper comes with paste applied to it, treat it as though it is unpasted. Don't soak it in water, but apply a coat of ordinary wallpaper paste and leave it to soak in before applying the paper to the wall.

PRODUCING A PROFESSIONAL FINISH

In addition to all the usual rules of wallpaper application, there are one or two extra procedures that can be carried out in bathrooms to give a totally professional finish. Follow the manufacturer's recommendations and make sure that the wallpaper has soaked for the appropriate time before applying it. Have all the wallpapering tools at hand before you start. Keep areas as clean as possible at all times and, above all, make sure that from the very first sheet the pattern is correctly joined and the paper is vertical.

2

Corners: apply the paper in the usual way, then peel back corner overlaps before they dry and apply some overlap or border adhesive along the entire corner junction before securing it back in place. This creates a doubly strong bond. Remove excess adhesive with a damp sponge.

Varnishing: non-vinyl papers can be varnished to give a protective coat to their finish. Some vinyl papers will accept varnish, but it is best to try a small test area first.

Windows: bathroom window recesses are prone to condensation, which will lift paper edges if not treated. Run a bead of waterproof caulking along the frame/paper junction to prevent any paper from lifting.

Baseboards: apply decorator's caulking along the baseboard/paper junction, allow it to dry, then paint the baseboard as usual. The caulking provides an extra seal and prevents the paper edges from lifting.

PAINT EFFECTS

C reating a good paint effect has as much to do with having the correct glaze mixture as the actual application. Nowadays, acrylic ready-mixed glazes are widely available; once mixed with colorizers, they are easy to apply and create stunning paint effects. Acrylic glaze is best applied over a water-based paint base coat—satin-finish latex paint provides the longest "working" time for the glaze on the wall.

2

COLOR-WASHING

Color-washing is one of the simplest effects to produce, giving an excellent finish which creates depth and texture on the wall surface. It is ideal on slightly rough plastered walls as it highlights this rustic feature and gives the room a relaxing, comfortable atmosphere.

1 Apply the glaze in all directions across the wall surface using an ordinary paintbrush. Work in areas of approximately one square yard (meter) so that the glaze does not dry out too quickly.

2 Rub a clean, slightly dampened cotton rag over the wall to remove the excess glaze, leaving the remnants to highlight any slight depressions in the painted surface. Rub off as little or as much of the glaze as you like, depending on the amount of color you want to leave on the wall.

CREATING ATMOSPHERE
Simple yet very effective, color-washing produces a great impact with relatively little skill required.

RAG ROLLING

Standard paint effects can be combined with other techniques to produce a more individual look in your bathroom. It can be very fulfilling trying out complex effects like rag rolling in the bathroom because the wall spaces are generally smaller than in other areas of the home and you can see the results of your efforts really quickly.

2

1 Apply a base coat to the wall and allow it to dry. Draw a number of equidistant vertical lines across the surface, making very light pencil marks. Run masking tape along each line edge to produce a masked-off, striped effect.

2 Have a number of rolled-up dampened rags at hand before applying the glaze to two or three of the masked-off areas. Do not apply glaze to all the masked-off areas at once as the glaze will dry before you can rag roll all of it.

3 Form a damp rag into a sausage shape and roll it down the wall through a glazed area. Change to a different rag for each stripe and rinse the rags between each new glaze application. Repeat the process until all the stripes are done, then remove the tape.

3

STRIPED EFFECT
Combining the austere, straight lines of stripes with a rag-rolled effect produces a wonderfully clean and refreshing look on a wall.

COMBINING PAINT EFFECTS

S ome paint effects complement each other really well and can be used together on a surface. Many of these effects require special tools that you need to practice using before you can achieve the best results. It is worthwhile building up a paint effect tool kit so that you can experiment with effects and produce finishes of your own design.

2

COMBING AND DRAGGING

Combing and dragging combine well as both have a pronounced texture that creates a very definite pattern on the wall surface. Both are suited to small areas—they can be overwhelming on large open surfaces. The paneled design shown here is an excellent compromise, reducing the amount of wall coverage of each effect while still producing a finish of considerable impact.

1

2

1 Mask off some equal-size panels on the wall, using floor tiles as a template. Measure a second panel inside the first, and mask off along its edges before glazing inside the panel with an ordinary paintbrush.

2 Starting at the top left-hand corner of the panel, make vertical sweeps down through the glaze using a graining comb.

3 After every second or third sweep with the comb, wipe the excess glaze from the comb with a dry cotton rag. Once the vertical sweeps have been completed, use the same technique to create horizontal sweeps across the entire panel.

3

4 Allow the glaze to dry, remove the masking tape, and apply more tape around the outside of the outer panel. Although it would be easier to mask off the internal combed panel, the tape can pull away the glazed surface when removed and a glazed surface can be difficult to touch-in. Apply glaze to the outer "frame," taking care not to get any on the internal combed area.

5 Use a fairly coarse-bristled brush to drag through the glaze along each side of the "frame." A dragging brush could be used, but they are generally much wider than the area allows. Angle the brush so that it is at a very acute angle with the wall surface, and make smooth, even sweeps in the glaze.

6 Make sure you create a definite "square" joint between each side of the frame, since precise finishing at corners adds to the effect. When the frame is complete, remove the masking tape. Continue with other panels, repeating Steps 1–6.

TEXTURED PANELING
This paneled effect is impressive in any room, but in a bathroom the matching shape of the tiles and the panels produces a very smart and well-integrated decorative scheme.

PAINTED SCENES

H and-painted scenes and expansive murals are difficult projects because they require considerable artistic talent. However, it is possible for anybody to use stencils and stamps to produce designs for small localized wall areas or for parts of a big picture.

STENCILS

Home decorating superstores and craft stores sell stencils to suit all tastes, but it can be very rewarding to make your own unique stencils. All you have to do is draw or trace a simple design, transfer it to a sheet of acetate, then carefully cut out the design to produce your own custom-made stencil.

| Lay a sheet of acetate on top of the drawn or traced design and use a fiber-tip pen to transfer the design onto the surface of the sheet.

2 Place the acetate on a cutting mat or an old scrap of building board. Using a craft knife, cut out the required sections of the design.

STENCILING

- Paint the design with rhythmic dabbing motions of the brush.
- As well as custom-made brushes, other tools can be used for stenciling designs, such as paint crayons and aerosol paints.
- Create depth by applying more paint to the outer edges of a stencil design—this produces a more three-dimensional effect. Building up color on one side of the design produces a shadow.

3 Secure the stencil with masking tape, then paint the design. Remove excess paint from the brush before each application and keep it perpendicular to the wall surface.

STAMPING

Stamps are an easy way of applying specific images to a wall surface. These can be homemade, but the process is very time consuming, especially when creating anything more than a simple, straightforward design. The growing popularity of stamping means that you can now buy a wide range of designs.

1 Spread paint evenly on the stamp with a brush or a custom-made foam roller. Apply the stamp to the wall surface, pressing down firmly to make sure all areas of the stamp are in full contact with the wall.

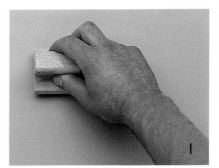

2 Lift the stamp carefully to avoid it sliding across the wall surface and smudging the paint. Vary the intensity of the image according to your personal taste by adjusting the amount of paint applied to the stamp and by removing excess paint from the stamp before applying it to the wall surface.

COMBINING EFFECTS

Stamps and stencils are ideal paint effects to combine on a wall, as each brings its own character to a painted scene. They can be used to make a variety of different scenes for the bathroom.

MULTICOLORED EFFECTS
The single color of stamps, mixed with the more broken, multicolored effect of stencils, creates a wonderful combination of color and design on this bathroom wall.

PROTECTING WORK

T he life expectancy of paint and wallpaper in the bathroom will always be less than in other areas of the home, but by carrying out a few extra tasks, this period can be lengthened considerably.

2

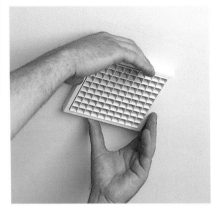

Dealing with moist air: the most significant damage done to bathroom surfaces results from lingering moist air and condensation. Inserting an effective exhaust fan in a bathroom is therefore the single most important task to carry out. Unfortunately, in most cases, it is not a particularly straightforward task and it is worth seeking professional advice for both positioning and fitting.

Polishing tiles: to prolong the life of tile grout, clean the tiled surfaces from time to time with a silicone-based polish. This gives the grout an extra seal to protect it and maintain its color.

Sealing effects: the glaze used for paint effects doesn't provide the most hard-wearing of finishes and it requires further protection, especially in a bathroom. Use a mat varnish or proprietary latex paint glaze coat on all paint effects. This will also give a surface that can be wiped easily.

RENOVATING FLOORS

Bathroom flooring is largely a matter of personal choice—whether you prefer the warm feel of carpet underfoot, or the water-repellent properties of hard tiles and vinyl. Most types of floorcovering are suitable, and, like any other decorative system, they have both advantages and disadvantages. However, the one consistent factor, which remains the same for any bathroom flooring, is its hardwearing capability—this must be considered thoroughly before making a final decision. This chapter explains the pros and cons of the different types of floorcovering and illustrates the best way of laying them.

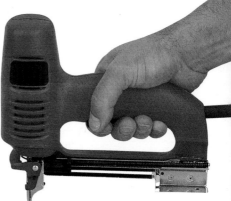

CHOOSING A STYLE

The floor style of your bathroom will almost certainly be directly affected by the decoration of the room—the paint, wallpaper, and tiles will all influence the final decision. Cost is also a relevant factor: although carpeting a floor may be cheaper than laying tiles, the carpet will need replacing more quickly. Also, in small bathrooms it may be possible to use vinyl scraps from other areas of the house, such as the kitchen. Alternatively, simply painting a wooden floor can produce a great effect at a relatively low cost.

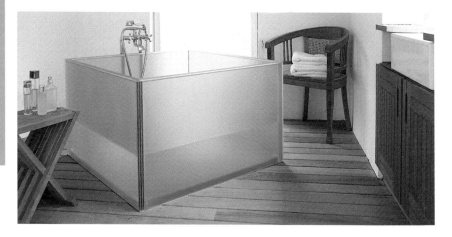

Keeping the wooden look: original wooden floors, or newly laid planking, provide a very natural, simplistic floorcovering that is relatively durable, as well as decorative. Such floors must be treated with the appropriate varnish or a coat of proprietary sealant to protect them from water attack.

The softer approach: carpets or natural floorcoverings, such as coir and seagrass, give a more cushioned feel underfoot than the harder alternatives. Using the same floorcovering in adjoining rooms gives a feeling of continuity and links the decoration as a whole.

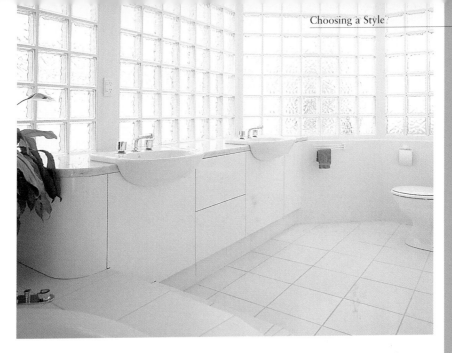

3

Tiling floors: solid and hardwearing, tiles produce an excellent finish in most bathrooms. It is essential that the correct technique is used when laying tiles, since mistakes can prove costly. Try and choose a design, whether extravagant or simple, that complements the surrounding decoration and gives a harmonious feel to the overall scheme.

Using paint: the easiest option can often be the most effective. Older floorboards, especially, benefit from a well-chosen paint color; as the floor ages and distresses, the overall look often improves. Proprietary floor paint is the professional choice, but less hardwearing paints can be used if a gradually aging and naturally distressed look is required.

RESTORING FLOORBOARDS

R estoring a planked floor to its former glory is a fairly arduous task, but the rewards are very worthwhile. Before old floorboards can be recoated with varnish, all old and ingrained coatings must be removed. For a small floor area, you can hire a sander to do this.

3

1 Use a hammer and punch to knock in any protruding nail heads on the floor before beginning to sand. Failure to do this will damage the sanding machine.

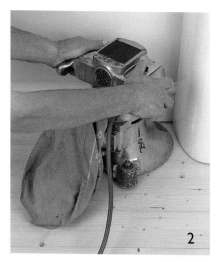

2 Edging sanders have orbital sanding heads that rotate and vibrate at the same time. Always follow the manufacturer's guidelines for use. Run the sanding machine back and forth over the floor surface, working with the grain. On the first sweeps with the sander, use rough abrasive paper then gradually work down to smoother grades. The whole floor should be sanded three or four times, progressively reducing the coarseness of the abrasive paper.

3 When the whole floor is sanded, vacuum up the sawdust and clean away the remnants with a rag dampened with mineral spirits. As soon as the mineral spirits have evaporated, the floor is ready to finish with varnish or sealant.

LARGE FLOORS

For large bathrooms, you need to rent a drum sander as well as an edger. The same technique of reducing the abrasive paper coarseness is used (see opposite), but a slightly more methodical work sequence is required to produce an evenly sanded surface. Follow the manufacturer's guidelines for use and always wear a dust mask. Always tilt the sander back before starting it, otherwise you may damage the floorboards while the sander is stationary but turned on.

First, sand at 45 degrees to the line of the floorboards.

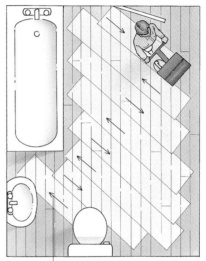

Next, sand at 45 degrees in the opposite direction.

3

Finally, sand with the grain of the boards.

Use overlapping sweeps with the sander.

Finish around the perimeter of the room with an edging sander.

HARDBOARDING A FLOOR

Hardboarding is a method of floor preparation that is used to cover floorboards before laying vinyl coverings, or where floorboards are old and uneven and a flat surface is required for laying carpet. Before hardboarding, make sure that any access to underfloor surfaces is not going to be covered over—install inspection hatches in the hardboard, if necessary.

1 Ensure that all floorboards are securely in place, screwing down any creaky boards before you cover them with hardboard. Make sure that you do not screw into any underfloor service wires or pipes.

2 Secure the hardboard in position, shiny side up, using a hammer and hardboarding nails or a custom-made staple gun. Small sheets of hardboard measuring 4 ft by 2 ft (120 cm by 60 cm) are the ideal size for bathrooms, since they are easy to maneuver. Stagger the edges of the hardboard sheets, so that no run of joins extends in a single line across the room. Secure the sheets every 6 in (15 cm) in all directions.

3 To cut hardboard sheets to fit smaller areas, use a craft knife and a straightedge, such as a spirit level, to score the hardboard. Turn the hardboard sheet over and snap the cut area upward so the sheet breaks along the scored line. It can then be fitted as normal.

CAUTION

Remember never to position your supporting hand in front of the craft knife blade when you are cutting the hardboard.

4 Use a paper template to cut around awkward areas. Cut slits in a sheet of paper, then mold it around the base of an obstruction such as a sink pedestal. Crease the slits into the profile of the pedestal and mark along the fold in the slits with a pencil.

5 Remove the paper, straighten out the slits, and cut along the pencil guideline to reproduce the exact profile of the pedestal. Hold the template on the hardboard and mark around the template with the pencil to indicate the shape to cut.

3

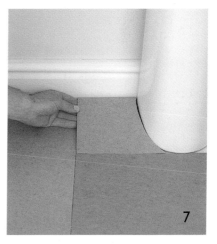

6 For cutting curves in hardboard, use a jigsaw rather than a craft knife, following the manufacturer's guidelines for using the saw, as well as their safety instructions.

7 Test the cut hardboard for shape around the obstacle before securing it in place.

DECORATING FLOORBOARDS

There are any number of different color and design possibilities for prepared floors: they can be given a traditional waxed finish or a varnished finish, or they can be painted or stained with equal effectiveness. It is possible to produce all kinds of unusual finishes by experimenting with colored stains and various paint effects, tailoring them to the needs of the room.

SIMPLE STAINING AND VARNISHING

Changing the natural wood color with stain and varnish is an easy way of altering the look of traditional floorboards. It is a relatively simple procedure as long as you follow the application guidelines below.

3

Keeping to edges: treat each floorboard as a separate unit when applying a stain. Try not to overlap the stain as this can lead to a very patchy finish that shows up brush marks rather than the natural grain of the wood. Work steadily across the floor, ensuring that a wet edge is constantly maintained between application strokes.

Going two-tone: a very effective decorative option for staining is to use two different colors and stain alternate floorboards. You can choose similar colors or a more definite contrast, as shown here. The technique of treating floorboards as separate units is clearly even more important in this case.

Protecting the finish: whatever the decorative finish, the floorboards must be varnished to protect it. Use a water-based varnish so that more than one coat can be applied in a day, and the bathroom can be back in use as soon as possible. Brush the varnish over the floorboards, carefully covering the whole area so the whole floor is protected.

FLOOR DISTRESSING

There are a number of ways of giving a distressed look to floorboards. One of the quickest and easiest is the technique demonstrated here, which uses two water-based latex paint colors to add interest to the finish. For the best result, make the second color darker than the first. Between the coats of paint, masking fluid is applied to random areas. This prevents the top coat of paint from adhering properly, and allows the bottom coat to show through. The overall effect is a colorful, distressed look.

1 Apply a base coat of latex directly onto the floorboards, working the paint into all areas. Allow it to dry.

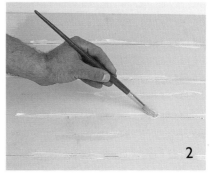

2 Apply small random streaks of masking fluid across the floor surface, paying particular attention to floorboard edges.

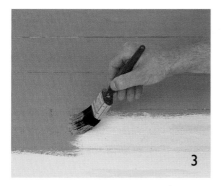

3 Paint a second color, preferably a darker color, across the entire floor surface. Allow it to dry before sanding the surface.

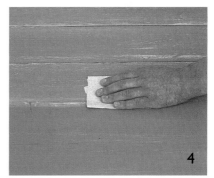

4 Sand the floor surface with fine grade abrasive paper. In the areas that had masking fluid applied to them, the bottom coat will show through. The floor can be varnished to protect it, or it can be allowed to distress further with general day-to-day wear and tear.

TILING THE FLOOR

H ard tiles are the most hardwearing of all bathroom floor options, but require some planning and preparation before application. They cannot be laid directly on floorboards; first, sheets of ¾-in (18-mm) plywood should be laid and secured to the floorboards to act as a base for the tiles. Once a secure and level base has been established, it is essential to plan the working sequence, making sure that the tiling is started in the correct place.

The bottom of the door may require planing since the tiles and plywood raise the floor level considerably.

Walls are rarely completely "square" in a room, therefore the baseboard can never be trusted as a straight guideline.

Position of first tile.

3

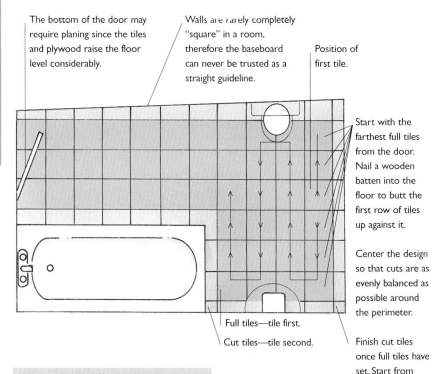

Start with the farthest full tiles from the door. Nail a wooden batten into the floor to butt the first row of tiles up against it.

Center the design so that cuts are as evenly balanced as possible around the perimeter.

Full tiles—tile first.

Cut tiles—tile second.

Finish cut tiles once full tiles have set. Start from farthest corner and work back to the door.

STARTING POINT

Rather than start in the corner of the room, position the first tile so that the distance to the walls on each side is equidistant. This way any cut tiles will be next to the walls, keeping the full tile design in the center of the room (see opposite page).

FLOOR TILING TECHNIQUE

Tiling floors is a methodical process, which is relatively straightforward as long as the floor has been well prepared. Fix a wooden batten to support the first row of tiles. It is best to use a flexible tile adhesive to deal with any slight floor movement when tiling on a suspended floor. Keep a constant check that tiles are laid level and gaps between tiles are kept consistent with tile spacers. Tiles can be cut with a standard tile cutter, which is normally strong enough to deal with most floor tiles. An electric tile cutter can be rented for particularly thick floor tiles, or for tiles in a bathroom that requires a lot of detailed cutting in order to tile around awkward shapes or other obstacles in the room.

1 Apply tile adhesive to the floor and lay the first tile tight against the supporting batten.

2 Cut tiles, as necessary, using a standard tile cutter or an electric tile cutter. If renting a cutter, follow the manufacturer's instructions for use and safety.

3 Apply adhesive directly to the back of the cut tiles and stick them in position. Leave to set.

4 Finish the surface with grout specifically designed for floor tiles. Use a grout spreader to press the grout into all tile joints. Remove excess grout from the tile surfaces before it sets, using a damp sponge.

LAYING VINYL FLOORING

Vinyl bridges the gap between hard tile floors and carpets. Hard-wearing and water-repellent, it makes an ideal bathroom flooring, which, although slightly cold underfoot, has a more cushioned feel than hard tiles but is not as soft as carpet. Sheet vinyl is tricky to fit, so take the time to measure and cut carefully to avoid mistakes.

MAKING A TEMPLATE

To get a roll of vinyl into a manageable size to fit in the bathroom, you need to make a template of the bathroom floor and transfer it onto the vinyl. This makes the trimming and fitting process much easier and allows for approximate positioning of the vinyl before it is finally secured in place.

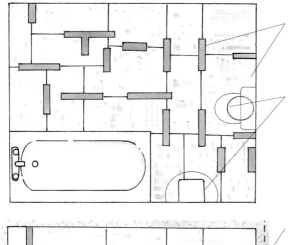

Use sheets of newspaper and masking tape to make an exact template of the bathroom floor.

Cut precisely around the pedestal edges.

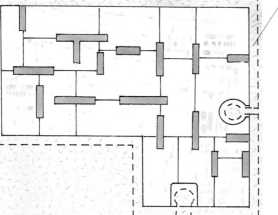

Place template on unrolled vinyl and cut around edge, adding 2 in (5 cm) onto the template size to allow for final fitting when positioned in the bathroom.

INSTALLATION GUIDELINES

Vinyl is not a totally flexible floorcovering because it will not stretch; therefore, accurate cutting is vital. Even the most experienced floor layers take extra time when laying vinyl, as it is very difficult to rectify mistakes once an incorrect cut has been made.

Straight lines: use a sharp craft knife to accurately cut straight edges next to baseboards. Crease the vinyl as firmly as possible into the floor/baseboard junction to ensure an accurate cut.

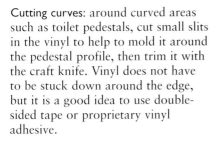

Cutting curves: around curved areas such as toilet pedestals, cut small slits in the vinyl to help to mold it around the pedestal profile, then trim it with the craft knife. Vinyl does not have to be stuck down around the edge, but it is a good idea to use double-sided tape or proprietary vinyl adhesive.

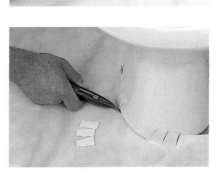

3

Joining: in larger bathrooms it may be necessary to join sheets of vinyl. In these cases, always join two factory-finished edges, and use double-sided tape to make sure that both pieces are stuck firmly to the floor.

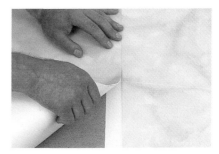

Extra sealing: because of the moisture in bathrooms, it is a good idea to run a bead of waterproof caulking around the perimeter of the vinyl to prevent water from seeping under it. For a neat finish, mask the floor/baseboard junction with two strips of masking tape, apply the caulking, then remove the tape immediately.

CARPETING FLOORS

C arpet provides the softest underfoot option for bathrooms, making it the most popular choice for many people. Carpets are easier to install than vinyl, although many of the techniques used in fitting are similar. There are two main types available: foam-backed carpets and the generally better quality burlap-backed carpets. There are small differences in laying the carpets, depending on which type you are fitting. Making a template of the floor (see page 66) is a good way of cutting carpet roughly to size before laying it.

FOAM-BACKED CARPETS

As the name suggests, foam-backed carpets are constructed so that the carpet fibers are joined directly onto a foam backing, which provides a cushioning layer designed to eliminate the need for underlay. These carpets tend to be less expensive, and easier to fit, than burlap-backed carpets. There is a large range of differing thicknesses and qualities available.

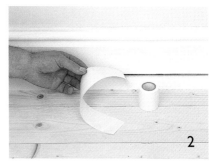

1 Trim the carpet to size with a craft knife, then remove it. Run double-sided carpeting tape around the perimeter of the room. .

2 Press the carpet edges firmly onto the tape to secure it in position on the floor.

SUBFLOOR IMPROVEMENT

Although foam-backed carpet has a cushioned effect, the quality of the carpet being laid and the evenness of the floor will determine how good the effect is. Rough floorboards or an uneven floor provide a poor base for carpet, unless you hardboard them first (see pages 60–61). Another simple way of improving the subfloor is to put down layers of newspaper as underlay.

BURLAP-BACKED CARPETS

Fitting burlap-backed carpets is a slightly lengthier process and involves the fitting of gripper strips to hold the carpet in place. Underlay is also required under the carpet to provide a cushioned feel underfoot. Underlay is supplied in rolls of various widths. It can be rolled directly onto the floor surface, trimmed to fit, then the carpet laid over the top.

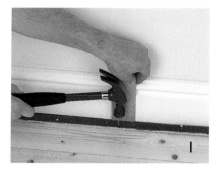

1 Secure gripper strips all the way around the perimeter of the floor. Make sure there is a small gap of ³⁄₁₆ in (5 mm) between the strips and the baseboard. Hold a piece of hardboard next to the baseboard to avoid scuffing it with the hammer when nailing the strips in place.

2 Cut some gripper strips into small sections to go around any curved edges such as the toilet pedestal. Once all the strips have been secured, roll out the underlay across the entire floor, making sure that it is laid to the edge of the gripper strips, but not over them.

3 Lay out the roughly shaped carpet, creasing it into the floor/baseboard junction, and cut to fit using a sharp craft knife. Use a carpet stretcher to totally flatten out the carpet surface, placing it under slight tension as it binds around the edges with the gripper strips.

4 Use a brick chisel to push the edge of the carpet over and behind the gripper strips to secure it firmly in position.

FLOORCOVERING CHECKLIST

I t can be useful to weigh all the pros and cons of the different floorcovering options before making a final decision about your bathroom floor. As well as taking into account the flooring techniques shown in this chapter, the good and bad points of the various floorings themselves will affect your decision.

PROS AND CONS OF BATHROOM FLOORING

FLOOR TYPE	Durability	Ease of cleaning	Preparation	Laying/ Finishing	Expense
	poor ✔ excellent ✔✔✔✔✔	difficult ✔ easy ✔✔✔✔✔	lengthy ✔ quick ✔✔✔✔✔	difficult ✔ easy ✔✔✔✔✔	high cost ✔ low cost ✔✔✔✔✔
Burlap-backed carpet	✔✔✔	✔✔✔	✔✔	✔✔✔	✔✔
Foam-backed carpet	✔✔	✔✔✔	✔✔✔	✔✔✔✔	✔✔✔✔
Vinyl flooring	✔✔✔✔	✔✔✔✔✔	✔✔	✔	✔✔
Stripped flooring	✔✔✔✔	✔✔✔	✔✔✔	✔✔✔✔✔	✔✔✔✔✔
Painted flooring	✔✔✔	✔✔	✔✔✔✔	✔✔✔✔✔	✔✔✔✔✔
Hard tile	✔✔✔✔✔	✔✔✔✔✔	✔	✔✔	✔

3

FIXTURES

The wallpaper and paintwork are not the only things that give a bathroom its decorative appeal. The fixtures that make the room fully functional are just as important. Lighting, bathtub screens, and window decorations

are just a few of the areas that need to be integrated into the overall design scheme to produce the desired finish. The number of fixtures will depend on both room size and personal requirements, but, regardless of the number, fixtures must be positioned correctly and secured in place as professionally as possible. Most of these tasks can be carried out by a practical amateur home decorator, though it may be necessary to seek professional help in some areas—if any electrical wiring is required, for example.

4

SHOWER AND BATHTUB SCREENS

S hower and bathtub screens are used to prevent splashes of water
from covering bathroom surfaces while the shower is being used. A
screen is required where a bathtub and shower are integrated—when
they are separate, a shower is more likely to have its own screen
housing. Whichever variety is suitable, most manufacturers supply
adequate, although varied guidelines for installation.

Bathtub screening: bathtub screens are
quite straightforward to install, and
clear glass varieties provide a
relatively unobtrusive mechanism for
containing a bathtub and integrated
shower. Many consist of two main
screens, one of which can slide out
across the bathtub rim to extend the
overall screen length and so prevent
any overspray onto the bathroom
floor when the shower is in
operation.

4

Shower cubicles: separate showers are
best housed in an enclosed cubicle to
prevent water from spraying over the
floor. Any number of designs and
screen shapes are available, but make
sure that your chosen screen fits the
shower tray dimensions. Access to
the shower can be by means of a
customized (watertight) hinged door,
or a sliding door similar to the
mechanism on bathtub screens.

INSTALLING AFTER TILING

If possible, fit a bathtub screen
before tiling the bathroom; if
installing after tiling, you will need to
use a tile drill bit to make holes in
the tiles for the screen fixings.

INSTALLING A BATHTUB SCREEN

Since the function of a bathtub screen is to create a watertight barrier, this must be the primary consideration when installing it—concentrate your efforts on keeping the screen completely vertical, easily operational, and fitted in the correct position according to the shower requirements. Make sure that the base of the retaining bracket sits central to thc bathtub rim so water will run down onto the rim and back into the bathtub once the screen is in place.

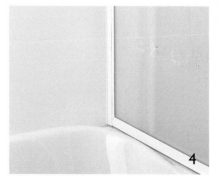

1 Use a long spirit level to ensure that the bathtub screen retaining bracket is positioned precisely vertical, and that the base sits central to the bathtub rim. Use a pencil to mark its position on the wall and also where the retaining screw holes should be drilled.

2 Remove the bracket, and drill holes ready to house the retaining screws. Depending on the wall surface and the method of fixing, wall anchors may be required. If this is the case, insert them at this stage, making sure that drill bit size, anchor size, and screw size all correspond.

4

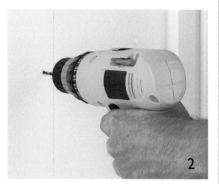

3 Hold the bracket back in place, checking that it is vertical once more, and screw the bracket in position on the wall.

4 Fit the screen into the bracket, following the manufacturer's guidelines. Apply caulking around the wall screen junction to provide a watertight seal.

MIRRORS

Mirrors are seen as one of the more essential bathroom fixtures, and it is rare to come across a bathroom that does not have at least one. As well as being used for practical purposes, mirrors can also be used decoratively—achieving different effects within specific bathroom surroundings. Size, shape, and style are all important considerations when adding mirrors to your bathroom.

4

Creating space: mirrors are perfect for creating an impression of greater space in a small room. They are particularly well suited to bathrooms, especially if you can have a large wall area of mirrors to enhance this reflective effect.

Being practical: remember that the main function of most mirrors is a practical one, and this should be taken into account when positioning them. However, practicality can be married with decorative appeal to produce all sorts of interesting effects.

Decorative priorities: where practicality is not the foremost concern, a mirror can be more of a decorative accessory—its style and position combining with other features in the room to enhance the overall decor. In some cases, the period or style of the mirror can add to the authenticity of the room's decorative scheme.

USING SCREW FIXINGS

Mirrors can be hung like pictures on hooks; for a flatter finish against the wall, they can be screwed in flush against the wall with specially designed screws that hold the mirror in place while providing an attractive, neat finish.

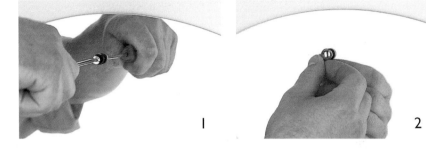

1 Drill holes in the wall for the number of screw fixings required. Fit wall anchors, if necessary, then insert small rubber rings into the holes in the mirror to stop it cracking when the screws are tightened. Tighten the screws, without overtightening them.

2 Insert dome-shaped covers over the mirror screws—they have a threaded core that is designed to have these covers screwed into it. The covers hide the screwheads and provide a more aesthetically pleasing finish to the mirror.

USING ADHESIVE

Some mirrors are not made with factory-drilled holes for attachment. These mirrors can be glued to the wall, with a proprietary mirror adhesive. The mirror must be supported on a wooden batten until the adhesive has set.

4

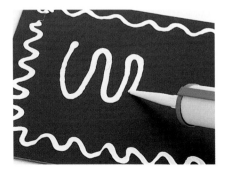

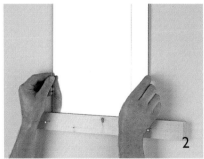

1 Nail a horizontal batten into the wall. Apply a generous amount of adhesive to the back of the mirror—a wavy line pattern ensures good suction when the mirror is bedded in position on the wall.

2 Position the mirror on the wall, resting it on the batten. Do not remove the batten until the adhesive has totally dried, otherwise the mirror may slip out of position, or fall off the wall and be damaged.

LIGHTING

L ight, whether natural or artificial, can have a profound effect on any bathroom scheme. It requires careful thought to decide what best suits the atmosphere of the room and its decoration, and it fulfills the practical requirements of the room. For safety reasons, electrical work should be carried out by a qualified electrician.

4

Focusing light: downlighting can be aimed directly at a certain part of the room so that a specific task can be carried out. Experimenting with varying levels of light can produce different moods while retaining the directional function.

DIRECTIONAL LIGHTING

Everyday bathroom activities necessitate light sources that are directional and can be used to clearly light up certain areas. This function may be included in the overall lighting setup in the room, but in many cases it can be confined to more direct-task lighting, designed to direct light exactly where you want it.

Even lighting: fluorescent tubes give good overall lighting. They can be used close to sinks and vanity units to provide excellent light consistency, and this effect can be exaggerated by the use of mirrors.

Downlighting: rather than aiming light at one particular part of the room, overall downlighting tends to give even light throughout the room, making all areas relatively consistent in terms of their light level.

Wall lighting: wall lights come in a large selection of styles and strengths. They give you the option of focusing light up or down, depending on personal requirements and mood preferences for the room.

Natural light: during daytime, natural light can produce a very invigorating and enlivening atmosphere. However, by the evening, this can change to a calmer feeling that can be enhanced by soft artificial light.

4

BATHROOM ACCESSORIES

B athroom accessories can transform the look of the room, so accessory style is an important design element. Whether the accessories are essential or optional, large or small, make sure that they blend with the room's decoration and add to its overall appeal.

TOWEL RAILS

Most bathrooms require something to hang towels on to dry, and heated towel rails are ideal for speeding up this process. The functional role of the towel rail can combine with the look of other accessories in the room—whether traditional, or more modern and innovative—to provide a well-integrated scheme.

Traditional rails: simple in construction and style, a traditional rail fits well into an established bathroom surrounding. Whether it is powered by electricity, or is part of the central heating system as shown here, a traditional towel rail is practical as well as smart.

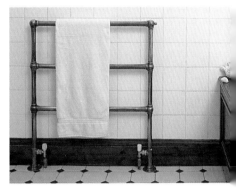

4

Modern systems: in recent years, rail designs have become more varied and innovative. Using the heat from radiators to dry out items on a fixed framework of rails is a way of extending the function of the radiator, while producing an unusual alcove design which fits well into a modern bathroom design.

CHANGING FIXTURES

All the smaller bathroom fixtures are quick and simple to change, making it easy to alter the appearance of wall surfaces. Bathroom makeovers do not have to be complex and time consuming to achieve a change in style.

Fitting the fixtures: many essential wall fixtures come supplied with a paper template that makes marking for drill fixings much easier. Simply position the template and mark the appropriate points on the wall.

The simplest of changes: cord pulls for lights or shades are often a neglected area of change. Many variations on the standard plastic theme are available, and can be attached in seconds.

DOOR LOCKS

Bathroom locking systems come in all manner of designs—choosing one is a matter of personal choice and what suits your bathroom. Locking systems that are separate to the handle mechanism are one option, although a fully integrated handle and locking system can often provide the neatest solution.

4

Operating the lock: integral systems work on a locking screw centrally positioned on the bathroom handle.

Child safety: the beauty of an integral system is that most can be opened from the outside with a special safety key. This means a trapped child can easily be freed with little fuss.

DECORATING BATHROOM ACCESSORIES

M ost bathroom accessories can be transformed with paint, varnish, and all manner of other standard decorating materials, whether you are renovating older items or starting from new.

NEW TOILET SEATS

One of the last outposts of mundane practicality has at last been reached by the modern world of design and progress. Toilet seat style, color, and finish are now as important a part of bathroom makeovers as any other fixture. The natural wood look is one option for a seat finish; it is very easy to recoat with varnish, giving it excellent life expectancy as well as attractive looks.

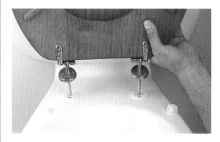

Installing seats: most seats are designed with universal fixtures that slot into the retaining holes at the back of the toilet bowl. These fixtures can be adjusted to fit the size of most toilets, but it is always worth checking that this is the case with your chosen design before you buy it.

RENOVATING AN OLD SEAT

4

Old plastic seats have little character of their own, but a quick change of color can integrate a seat into a specific bathroom scheme. Remove the seat before painting to protect the bowl and allow access to all areas of the seat itself.

1 Plastic seats need to be cleaned thoroughly before painting, using a proprietary surface preparation solution. This should be wiped onto the seat and then polished off to remove all dirt.

2 Spray the seat with several coats of acrylic paint, keeping the aerosol about 6 in (15 cm) from the seat surface. Work in smooth sweeping movements, applying several thin coats rather than a few thick ones. Follow the manufacturer's guidelines on aerosol safety; at the very least, you will need to wear a respiratory mask.

2

BATHROOM CHAIRS

Room for furniture is often severely limited in bathrooms because of their size; however, there is often space for the odd item, such as a bathroom chair. These can be used as a movable decorative item, which can either complement the surrounding decoration or provide a contrast. Aerosol paint effects, such as crackle glaze, are ideal for painting awkwardly shaped items.

1 Sand down the chair surface, and use a damp cloth to wipe off any dusty residue. Holding the aerosol about 6 in (15 cm) from the chair surface, work across the chair. Turn the chair around and then over to reach all the less accessible areas.

2 Allow the glaze to dry and the crackle effect to develop. When it is dry, spray the entire chair with a protective aerosol varnish.

4

THE AGED EFFECT
The crackle glaze on this chair provides a wonderfully aged look, which would look good in almost any bathroom scheme.

WINDOW SHUTTERS

W indows can be a problem area when decorating bathrooms since the choice of window dressings is frequently limited by the amount of available space. There may not be enough room for curtains, so producing a finish that ties in with the rest of the decoration can be difficult. Window shutters are an attractive option since they do not take up much room and can be very effective when limited to half the overall window size, in a café-curtain style.

I Measure the exact width and height of the window recess to establish the required dimensions of the shutters.

4

2 Make the two doors out of fretwork paneling by cutting the panel to the exact size of the doors, allowing in the measurements for two lengths of 2-by-1-in (5-by-2.5-cm) wooden batten to be positioned on each side of the window recess for hinging the shutter doors.

3 Attach four lengths of 2-by-½-in (5-cm-by-12-mm) batten all around the perimeter of each cut fretwork panel, using brads.

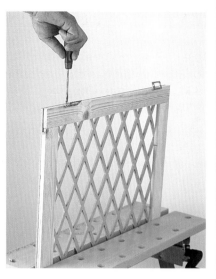

4 Cut two 2-by-1-in (5-by-2.5-cm) lengths of batten to exact door height and fix them securely on each side of the window recess.

5 Attach two hinges to each fretwork panel door.

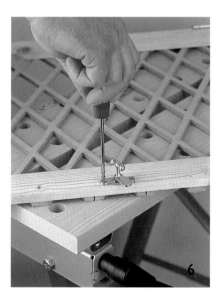

4

6 Attach a lever catch to the center of the doors.

7 Mark and attach the hinges onto the lengths of batten on each side of the window recess. Paint the shutters, and staple fabric to the inside of the panels for extra privacy.

FITTING BLINDS

B linds are a popular window treatment for bathrooms since they take up little room, can be highly decorative, and are easy to fix in place. As a window dressing, blinds always produce an excellent finish in bathrooms. More elaborate blinds, such as Austrian and festooned types are not included here; although they can be used in bathrooms, moisture lingers in the folds of material, making them prone to damp.

Window shades: these are the easiest way of controlling the flow of natural light into a room. Plain or highly patterned, they can fit well into most schemes. Because they can be rolled up completely onto their retaining pole, it means that the window can be totally exposed during the day so that the maximum amount of light can be let in, which is ideal for small or dark rooms.

Roman blinds: these operate by the material being gathered upward in folds as the blind is opened. They are slightly more complicated than rolling window shades, but if plain colors are used they can have a great effect on a simple scheme.

Venetian blinds: these have always had a classical appeal because of the unique way in which they break up the natural light source in a variety of mood-creating ways, as well as providing total privacy when the slats are closed at night.

4

NO-SEWING BLINDS

It is easy to create different types of blinds very quickly, without even the hint of any complex stitching. Making a simple blind from some favorite material has never been easier, especially since the invention of hook-and-loop tape.

1 Measure the exact dimensions of the window frame. Make sure the width measurements come in fractionally from the wall recesses so that the finished blind will be able to fall easily at the frame edge. Add 6 in (15 cm) onto the height measurement to allow 3 in (7.5 cm) at each end of the blind for attaching a length of wooden dowel. Mark the material, and cut it to size using dressmaker's scissors.

2 Cut two lengths of wooden dowel to slightly less than the window recess width and place one at each end of the cut material. Fold over the material at one end and secure it in this position with self-adhesive hook-and-loop tape. Apply the corresponding side of the hook-and-loop tape 3 in (7.5 cm) farther onto the material. Apply two more strips of tape in corresponding positions at the other end of the material (on each side of the other batten). Fold the tape over each batten.

3 Screw two hooks into the window frame, in order to support one of the battens. The other batten is used to weigh down the blind and keep the material taut.

THE STITCHLESS LOOK
The simplest of blinds can often produce the most attractive effect. Here, the blend of colors and the intensity of the light combine to give the window a stylish finish.

PAINTING BLINDS

The easiest way of renovating old blinds, or brightening up cheap ones, is to decorate them with a design of your own choosing. Although a number of techniques can be used to make these decorative additions, paint and fabric are the most appropriate materials to use. Rolling window shades provide the best base for decoration as they are flat and they roll out into one complete "sheet," which makes them very easy to work on.

Stenciling blinds: this is one of the quickest ways of decorating a blind. Make sure that the stencil is held firmly in place when working on fabric since mistakes are quite difficult to rectify. Mask off the area immediately above and below the stencil run, to protect it from paint-covered hands when moving the design along to the next position.

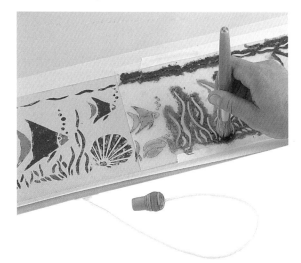

4

DECORATIVE TECHNIQUES

- Using paint: fabric paints should be used on blinds, although some acrylics are multipurpose and can be used on fabric as well as walls and other surfaces. This gives the opportunity to match paint colors and texture directly between different surfaces. Stencils and stamps work particularly well on blinds, and this method of painting them also allows designs to be carried over from wall to fabric surface, creating an integrated decorative scheme in the room.

- Using fabric: cutting out different shapes or designs and using fabric glue to stick them to a plain blind is another decorative option. This technique, known as appliqué, can be very effective in transforming the look of a simple blind.
- Design tracing: colorfast ink pens are ideal for hand-drawn designs on fabric. For the less artistic, a design traced from a book or a picture can be used to excellent effect. Iron the back of the blind to "fix" the ink once the design is finished.

ESSENTIAL PLUMBING

Household plumbing has always been considered the domain of the professional, and this sentiment remains unchallenged for the majority of plumbing tasks around the home. However, there are some tasks that can be carried out without too much trouble: this chapter demonstrates the areas of plumbing that fit into this band of manageable jobs—home maintenance jobs, or tasks that involve changing fixtures for a new-look bathroom. Plumbing systems vary considerably, depending on age and size requirements, so the examples given here deal with principles rather than trying to cover every eventuality. Approach plumbing work with an open mind and decide which areas you are capable of tackling and which areas should be left to the professional.

PLUMBING TOOLS

Never make compromises on plumbing tools, since the correct ones are essential for achieving the right result. In addition to a general tool kit, the household plumber needs a few extra items. Most of these can be found in home improvement centers: however, for some items you may need to go to a store for professionals—the bonus of this is being able to get advice from the experts.

Hole saw
For cutting pipe-size holes through walls.

Pipe cutter
Makes cuts through copper or plastic pipe.

Plumbing tape
Makes threaded joints watertight.

Long-nosed pliers
Ideal for detailed work in awkward places.

Pipe bender
For bending small diameter copper pipes.

Pipe wrench
Has movable jaws to grip onto most sizes of pipe.

Adjustable pliers
Has movable jaws for maximum gripping strength.

5

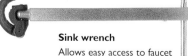

Sink wrench
Allows easy access to faucet connectors below sink.

Gas torch
For soldering pipe joints.

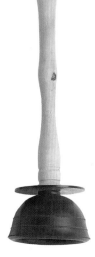

Plunger
For unblocking toilets and waste pipes.

CHOOSING A STYLE

The style of faucet and shower fixtures for a bathroom is always a matter of personal taste, though it is heavily influenced by whether the bathtub and shower are integrated or separate, and whether the bathroom design suits one particular type of fixture better than another. When an entirely new bathroom is being installed, most stores supply a good range of matching plumbing fixtures. Decision-making is slightly more difficult when renovating an old bathroom.

Choosing a shower: showers vary considerably in price, which is due as much to design as it is to their efficiency. Make sure that the controls are simple to use and hard-wearing, and check whether the shower itself requires a complicated installation procedure, as this will increase the cost.

Sink faucets: faucets come in all sizes and shapes, with modern or more traditional ones being equally popular in most stores. Always try and match the sink faucet style with those of the bath, and remember to check that the new faucets you choose will fit your sink.

Integrated systems: where the bathtub and shower are integrated, a simple option is to choose an old-fashioned faucet with the showerhead resting on a bracket above the handles. Another bracket for the showerhead can be attached to the wall to allow hands-free showering.

5

CHANGING FAUCETS

O nce all the relative checks have been made to ensure that the new faucets will fit your plumbing, exchanging them for the old ones is a relatively easy procedure. Faucets are literally secured onto the end of the water pipes by simple connectors: changing them is just a matter of unscrewing these connector joints to remove the old faucets, fitting the new faucets in place, then screwing the connectors back in place.

1 Once the water supply is shut off, take off the water supply pipe to gain access to the back nut on the faucet. Use a sink wrench to undo the nut at the top of the supply pipe, which connects the pipe to the faucet above.

2 With the water pipe removed, undo the faucet's back nut. Repeat the process to disconnect the water pipe to any other faucets. The faucets are now free to be removed from above and new faucets installed. Depending on faucet design, it may be necessary to disconnect the pop-up rod for the waste pipe. This is normally a simple matter—check the manufacturer's guidelines to see whether a new sink stopper needs to be installed.

CAUTION

Before any faucet can be installed, the water supply must be turned off. Most modern water systems have shutoff valves that are situated close to the faucets themselves— often they are a short way along the faucet supply pipes below the sink. The sink faucets can then be turned on to drain off the small amount of water left in the end section of the pipe.

5

INSTALLING THE NEW FAUCETS

Washers or silicone should be used to cushion faucet block onto the sink surface. Check manufacturer's guidelines for the faucets you are using.

Faucet tails should be lowered through the appropriate holes.

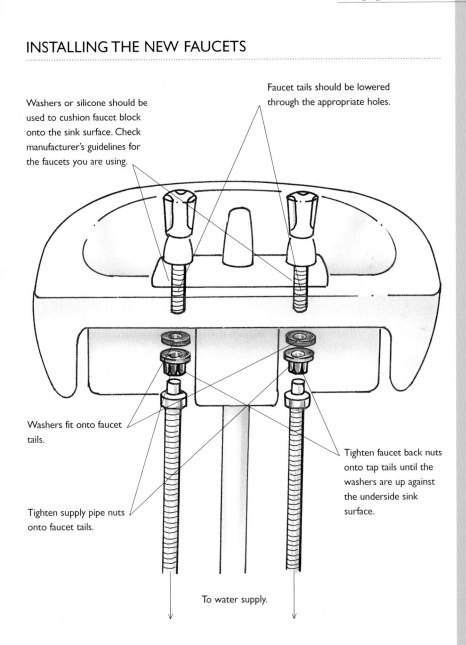

Washers fit onto faucet tails.

Tighten faucet back nuts onto tap tails until the washers are up against the underside sink surface.

Tighten supply pipe nuts onto faucet tails.

To water supply.

5

(Only turn on water when all joints are tightened.)

DEALING WITH LEAKING FAUCETS

L eaky faucets are a frequent and annoying problem in bathrooms. Fortunately, they are usually an easy problem to fix, and one that takes little time and expense. The most common cause of a leaking faucet is a broken or corroded washer, or one with a hairline crack. No matter what the faucet design, the water must be turned off at the shutoff valve (stopcock) that feeds the faucet. The faucet can then be opened to drain off any water in the pipe system. Only when this is done, can you work on the faucet to replace its washer.

REMOVING THE FAUCET HEAD

Designs vary, but in most cases the actual faucet head is held on by a small setscrew, which can be undone to release the head. The screw may be hidden by a cover cap, as shown below. Once the head is removed, the internal workings are revealed. Some faucets will have an extra cover, or shroud, that will need to be unscrewed before you can replace the washer.

1 Prize off the cover cap with a straight-bladed screwdriver, and undo the retaining screw that holds the faucet head in place.

2 The washer is still hidden by the headgear of the faucet. Use an adjustable wrench to grip the headgear nut and undo it slowly to remove the headgear. If the nut does not move easily and greater effort is required, make sure that you support the rest of the faucet mechanism with your other hand to avoid damaging any of the faucet parts.

CHANGING THE WASHER

Once the headgear has been removed, the washer can be clearly seen, and replacing it is straightforward. In some cases, the old washer can be prized directly off the bottom of the headgear; in the example below, a small fixing nut is used to hold the washer in place.

1 Undo the fixing nut with long-nosed pliers. Because this nut is so small, it is easily lost so be sure to put it in a safe place before refitting.

2 Carefully prize out the damaged washer with a straight-bladed screwdriver.

3 Clip in a new washer, making sure that it is the correct size, and fits tightly in position. Refit the fixing nut, and screw the headgear back into the main faucet body. Once the faucet head is back in place, close the faucet before turning the water supply back on. If the washer has been installed correctly, the drip will be cured.

5

ADJUSTING TOILET TANKS

The main problems found with toilet tanks either involve constantly dripping overflow pipes, or insufficient water to expel all material from the bowl when the toilet is flushed. Both cases are linked to the water level in the tank; this is easily adjustable since nearly all tank levels are based on the same system, built around an air-filled float. This float rises and falls with the water level, shutting a valve to prevent water from flowing into the tank when the water level is high, and opening the valve when water level is low (after flushing). The air-filled float is positioned on the end of an arm, and there are two main methods of adjusting the level at which the arm shuts off the incoming water flow.

Traditional ball cocks: traditional air-filled floats, often called ball cocks, can be adjusted by bending the metal arm so that the ball cock changes its level in the water. Alternatively, as shown here, its height can be adjusted by loosening a small nut, which then allows the ball cock to be moved up and down a small vertical stretch of the arm, again changing its level in the water.

Plastic arms: some air-filled floats are held in position with plastic arms. In this case, adjustment tends to be at the other end of the arm, close to the valve controlling water flow. These arms are normally adjusted by using long-nosed pliers to change the position of a small nut on the arm, which increases or decreases the level at which the air-filled float will shut off the water supply to the tank.

5

BATHTUB WASTE SYSTEMS

B athtub waste systems vary considerably, but most are based on a design which takes water out of the bathtub through a U-bend or trap and out into the main sewage system. Blockages and leaks occur because of problems in this simple system. Dealing with any problems is relatively simple as long as you understand the way in which such systems interconnect. This diagram shows a standard bathtub waste system and the areas that can cause potential problems.

BATHTUB WASTE SYSTEM

Leakages can be caused by:

Holes or corrosion of the overflow seal. The solution is to unscrew the overflow outlet system and run a bead of silicone around the overflow hole, before repositioning the overflow outlet system.

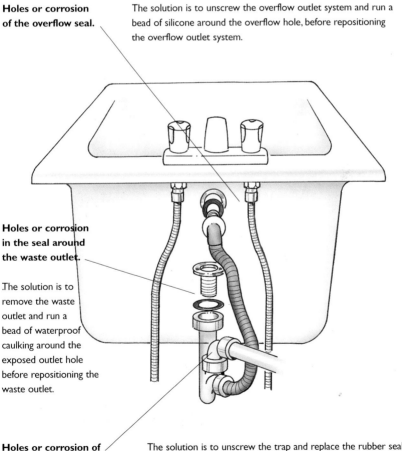

Holes or corrosion in the seal around the waste outlet.

The solution is to remove the waste outlet and run a bead of waterproof caulking around the exposed outlet hole before repositioning the waste outlet.

Holes or corrosion of the trap seals. The solution is to unscrew the trap and replace the rubber seals, or use waterproof caulking sealant around the thread of the trap pipes, before screwing the trap back in position.

5

GENERAL MAINTENANCE

T here are many simple plumbing jobs that come under the heading of general maintenance, and these small tasks can help to keep the main elements of the bathroom functioning efficiently. Problems occur when water is either not flowing at all, or not flowing as well as it should be, and this can be the water going into the bathroom or the water coming out of it.

DESCALING A SHOWERHEAD

Most shower flow problems result from the showerhead becoming blocked with mineral deposits—this is particularly common in areas with hard water. Fortunately, there is a simple way of clearing this problem and returning the showerhead water flow back to its proper efficiency level.

1 Unscrew the showerhead to remove the perforated plate.

2 Wearing protective gloves, scrub the plate with some descaling fluid using an old toothbrush. If it is badly blocked up, soak the entire plate in a bowl of descaling fluid overnight. Rinse the plate thoroughly after it has been in contact with descaling fluid.

3 Use a pin to remove any small deposits in the perforations of the plate, but do not use this method if the plate has an integral plastic diaphragm, as this could be damaged by a pin. Reassemble the showerhead to see if waterflow has improved.

5

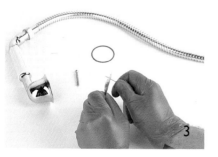

UNBLOCKING TOILETS

Toilets are one of the more common bathroom outlets that become blocked from time to time. As soon as you notice that flushing is less efficient than normal, or waste is not being carried away with the usual ease, it is likely that a blockage is building up. It is always best to rectify the problem right away—leave the blockage too long and major work will almost certainly be required. The solution is usually very simple.

Using a plunger: a simple plunger can often deal with minor blockages. Push it down into the bottom of the toilet bowl and plunge the handle up and down vigorously to create suction between the plunger head and the sides of the bowl. This puts water pressure on the blockage in the pipe and eventually moves it out of the way.

SINK WASTE

It is worth clearing sink waste traps from time to time since they do become blocked with small bits of debris and a buildup of silt. The design of the waste pipe does vary, but in general there are obvious areas in the trap that are meant to be unscrewed to dispose of any debris and dirt buildup.

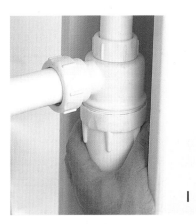

1

2

1 Unscrew the trap, taking care not to twist the rest of the outlet pipe structure and risk fracturing any of the seals.

2 The bottom of the trap should contain water but it ought to be relatively clean. If the water is dirty or there is debris at the bottom, clear it out, then screw back the trap.

5

QUICK SOLUTIONS

With plumbing systems, it is always good to know how the basic system works; that way, when there is a problem, the correct course of action can be taken to put it right. In some cases, you will need to call in the professionals, but there are other situations where you may be able to solve the problem yourself.

SOLVING PROBLEMS

- Corroded nuts: if you are trying to undo any pipe joints that are particularly stiff, try loosening them with some proprietary aerosol easing spray.
- Cold radiator: if a water-filled radiator in the bathroom is not giving off much heat, it is possible that the thermostat is turned down too low or is broken. Before replacing it, bleed the radiator to check that there is no air trapped in the system, preventing the radiator from warming up. In a pressurized central heating system, take care when bleeding radiators as it may be necessary to build the pressure back up in the system once it has been bled. Check your boiler instructions to see if this is the case.
- Frequent washer trouble: when washers on faucets keep giving trouble, it can be due to excess water pressure. Try turning down the stopcock slightly to reduce this pressure.
- Water too hot or cold: all water heating systems have a controlling

thermostat. Temperature problems with hot water can normally be traced to the thermostat, which should be adjusted as required. Check your heating installation instructions for detailed advice on thermostatic control in your system.
- Testing stopcocks: in emergencies, it may be necessary to turn off the water supply. It is vital to test stopcocks from time to time to check that they are functioning correctly; otherwise, when an emergency does arise, it may not be possible to turn the water off.
- Knowing a plumber: plumbers are well-trained professionals, and most plumbing jobs should be left to them. Find a plumber through personal recommendation, and keep the phone number handy for both emergencies and advice. Always remember that if you are in any doubt about attempting a plumbing job, it is best to call a professional.

5

BATHTUB AND SHOWER FIX-UPS

The bathtub and shower are often neglected in a bathroom makeover because there is a feeling that, apart from replacement, there is not much that can be done to improve them. This chapter demonstrates that there are, in fact, all sorts of changes that can be made to these bathroom fixtures, whether for decorative or practical purposes. After all, looking after bathtubs and showers has an important effect on maintaining the decorative impact of the bathroom as a whole. Finally, the ornamental aspects of decorating—those finishing touches that make a bathroom makeover complete—are considered at the end of the chapter.

TONGUE-AND-GROOVE PANELING: 1

MAKING THE FRAME

Before a bathtub can be paneled, you need to build a frame onto which the paneling can be attached. Use 2-by-1-in (5-by-2.5-cm) wooden battens for this purpose since they are sturdy enough to provide a sound base while being easy to work with. For the best results, build a frame that combines vertical and horizontal struts, with supporting diagonal lengths to brace the entire framework and keep it firmly in position.

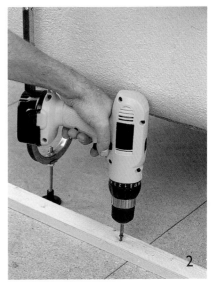

1 Cut a scrap of board the same thickness as the paneling you are going to use, to the height of the bathtub so that it just fits under the bathtub rim. Lay a piece of 2-by-1-in (5-by-2.5-cm) batten along the floor, parallel with the bathtub rim. Use a level and the board scrap to adjust the position of the batten so that it lies directly below the bathtub rim. Make a pencil guideline all the way along the batten.

2 Cut the batten to the length of the bathtub, and screw it into the floor, using screws that are long enough to bite into the floorboards below, but not so long that they might go through the boards and damage any service pipes and wires below the floor, and, more importantly, injure you.

6

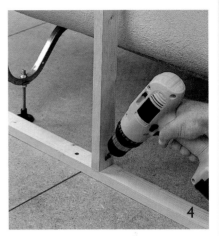

3 Measure the height from tight under the rim of the bathtub to the top of the floor batten. Cut four or five pieces of batten to this length, for vertical supports. Some bathtubs have a horizontal batten fixed under the rim, but it may be necessary to wedge another length of batten under the rim for fixing on vertical battens.

4 Attach the vertical battens at equal distances along the length of the bathtub, securing at floor level and under the rim. When attaching below the bathtub rim, be careful not to screw into the bathtub itself.

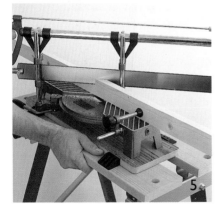

5 Use a miter saw to make angled cuts in another four or five pieces of batten to use as diagonal supports. Take care when measuring these mitered lengths to fit, as they must be accurate in order to keep the frame in the correct position for attaching the paneling.

6 Secure the diagonal batten supports between all the vertical lengths of batten on the frame.

6

TONGUE-AND-GROOVE PANELING: 2

O nce the panel frame has been made, the paneling itself must be cut to fit. Using large sheets makes the job quicker, but cutting accurately is that much more important, since small measurement mistakes in one area can lead to a larger mistake in another. Take time to measure carefully.

ATTACHING THE PANEL

When measuring the tongue-and-groove paneling, remember that the panel should fit just under the rim of the bathtub. Do not cut the paneling too large or you will not be able to get it under the rim.

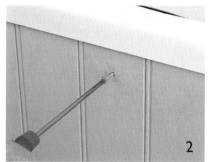

1 Use a jigsaw or panel saw to cut the bathtub panel to size. Once in position, drill six pilot holes in the panel, one at each corner, one in the center of the panel at the top (as shown here), and one in the center of the panel at the bottom.

2 Screw a mirror screw into each of the pilot holes. For a totally professional finish, before inserting the mirror screw, make each hole entrance slightly larger with a countersink drill bit, so that the screwhead will sit flush with the surrounding panel surface.

3 Attach a mirror screw cap to each screw. (Always remove mirror screw caps before painting the paneling and replace them once the paint has dried.)

6

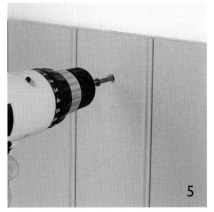

4 For the rest of the bathtub border, attach paneling as required. Using paneling the same height as the bathtub panel itself produces a well-balanced effect. Drill pilot holes every 8 in (20 cm) along the top and bottom of the paneling.

5 Use a countersink drill bit to open up the entrance to each hole before securing the panel. Concrete anchor screws, which bite equally well into wood or masonry, are shown here. If you are using normal screws, insert wall anchors before screwing in the screws.

DECORATIVE BATHTUB BORDERS
Once painted, a tongue-and-groove paneling provides a decorative and hardwearing bathtub border.

6 Finally, attach a length of quadrant beading around the top of the paneling to provide a smooth finish to the edge. Decorate, then seal the bathtub edge with caulking.

6

SHOWER CEILINGS

S hower ceilings are always under constant attack from moisture and can, therefore, deteriorate very quickly after painting. Tiling a ceiling is one way of getting around this problem, although gravity makes this a difficult task to achieve. Alternatively, a sheet of plastic (PVC) can be cut to fit the ceiling area, providing an easily cleaned, moisture-resistant surface that will not deteriorate like a painted one.

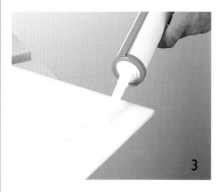

1 Measure the area directly above the shower, whether it be in a cubicle or above a bathtub.

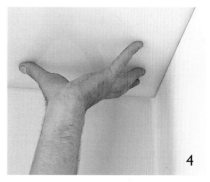

2 Cut a sheet of plastic to size, using a jigsaw. Remember to follow manufacturer's guidelines on safety when using a jigsaw, and at no time place any part of your body in front of the blade.

3 Apply a generous amount of silicone adhesive to the back of the sheet, making sure that there is plenty of adhesive at the edges.

4 Press the sheet into position above the shower, twisting it into place to ensure good adhesion between the sheet and the ceiling.

6

5 Some screw fixings are required to attach the sheet securely. Drill pilot holes around the edge of the sheet at 8-in (20-cm) intervals, being careful when drilling into the ceiling not to damage service pipes or wires, and, more importantly, not to risk injury to yourself.

6 Insert the screws and fit plastic screw cover caps over them to give a neat finish. Apply a band of silicone around the edge of the sheet to ensure a watertight finish.

DEALING WITH DAMP AND CONDENSATION

Damp and condensation can be a problem in bathrooms—the hot water from showers and bathtubs is the main cause of this problem. An exhaust fan is the best method of removing moist air from a bathroom (see page 54), but there are other measures that can also help.

- After a bath or shower, simply opening windows helps to reduce the moisture content of the air in the bathroom.

- Wiping off the moisture on walls helps to prevent the development of mold, which will always attack the decorations and lead to a rapid deterioration in their finish.
- Use proprietary bathroom paints that are more resistant to moisture than standard varieties.
- If your windows are single paned, consider installing double glazing since this will reduce condensation.
- Keep the room adequately heated.

6

RE-ENAMELING A BATHTUB

R e-enameling a bathtub sounds like a daunting task, and, until recently, this would have been a fairly accurate sentiment, since there were no easy-to-use systems available for carrying out this recoating process. However, the situation has changed and various proprietary products are now available. Before trying one, make sure that the new enamel coating is suitable for your bathtub—most should only be used on previously enameled surfaces or porcelain ones.

1 Mask all faucets and other fixtures on the bathtub, using plastic drop cloths. This has two functions: firstly, it keeps the faucets clean and, secondly, it stops any enamel drips from falling on the bathtub surface.

2 Use an electric sander to rub down the entire bathtub surface. Use the finest grade abrasive paper, as you do not want to make deep cuts in the bathtub surface. Wear a respiratory mask while carrying out this process.

3 Clean the bathtub surface thoroughly with a mild detergent, then rinse with clean water. Leave the bathtub to dry completely before finally wiping over the surface with a rag dampened with mineral spirits. This evaporates quickly to leave a totally clean bathtub surface ready for painting. Mask off the surrounding bathtub area with some masking tape.

6

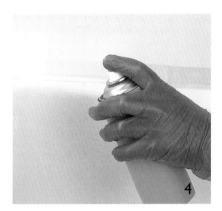

4 Use proprietary bathtub enamel to spray even coats over the entire bathtub surface. Wear a respiratory mask while applying the enamel. Manufacturers' guidelines vary, but normally three or four thin coats will produce a good finish. Allow plenty of drying time between the coats. Remove the masking tape when the last coat has dried.

BATHTUB RESTORATION
Re-enameling is particularly appropriate for older roll-top bathtubs that have suffered surface deterioration over the years. Restoring them to their original look can be a very satisfying process. The process does not have to be confined to bathtubs—sinks and shower trays can be re-enameled as long as they have a suitable surface.

TOUCHING-IN

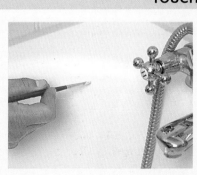

In many cases, re-enameling the bathtub is too extreme a measure, especially if the damage is slight. Any small nicks or scrapes in the surface can normally be touched-in very effectively with a small paintbrush, using the appropriate color of oil-based eggshell-finish paint. It may be necessary to add an extra coat, since it is better to apply two thin coats than one thick one.

6

CAULKING

Caulking seals are the vital barriers that prevent any water from getting through joints and cracks around all the bathroom fixtures. They help to prevent damp problems that could affect the decoration in other rooms in the house, such as leaking water from the bathtub area seeping through the floor and causing a damp patch on the ceiling of the room below the bathroom.

REMOVING OLD SEALS

Before a new seal can be applied, the old one must be removed. The total removal of the old seal is as important as the application of the new one in ensuring a watertight finish. Leaving any of the old seal will create weak areas in the new one.

1 Cut away the old caulking seal using a windowpane scraper. Concentrate your efforts with the corner of the scraper along the seal itself, being careful not to scratch the bathtub surface. Proprietary removal fluid can be used to help the process.

2 Clean the tile/bathtub junction with mineral spirits, allowing it to evaporate before applying a new seal.

1

2

CARING FOR SEALS

Resealing is part of the maintenance process for a bathroom, but the life of seals can be extended by wiping them off after a shower or bath to prevent damage from standing water.

6

CREATING THE NEW SEAL

With a clean junction between the bathtub and the tiles, applying the new seal is relatively straightforward. Make sure that the diameter of the sealant nozzle is cut to a size slightly larger than the bathtub/tile junction.

1 Apply strips of masking tape to each side of the bathtub/tile junction. Run the caulking gun along the junction, keeping an even pace as this makes smoothing it much easier.

2 Use a wet finger to run along the new caulking seal to create an uninterrupted smooth finish.

3 Remove the masking tape immediately after smoothing the caulking—do not wait until the caulking is dry before removing it.

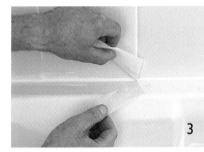

ALTERNATIVE SEALS

Seals are not confined to just white tubed caulking; other alternatives may be used either for decorative or practical reasons.

- Colors: a simple change is to substitute a different color for the existing white seal. This color can complement tiles or other colors in the bathroom.
- Double caulking: where a joint is particularly large, one application of caulking may not be enough to seal the gap effectively and neatly. Make one application to fill the deep recesses of the joint, allow it to dry, then make another application—the seal will then be easier to mold into a good finish.
- Plastic seals: in areas that cause constant damp problems, you can combine plastic strip seals with caulking. Apply generous amounts of caulking sealant to the joint before applying the plastic seal over the top.

6

FINAL FIX-UPS

No bathroom makeover is complete without ornaments and all the other decorative accessories that combine to create the finished look of a new room. The decorative accessories are really a matter of personal preference, determined by the style of the room—generally speaking, plants, pictures, and rugs are the favored items. Candles are becoming an increasingly popular form of decoration, not just for bathrooms, since they can create mood through their subtle lighting and, if you use scented ones, a wonderful aroma.

PLANTS

Indoor plants bring a fresh, natural atmosphere to any room. Several plants can be clustered together or you can have a single plant with interesting foliage or bold flowers. Plants can even be chosen to complement or blend with other colors in the decorative scheme of the bathroom.

PICTURES

Your choice of pictures in the bathroom can add to the decorative effect and personalize the room. Groups of pictures or single paintings create focal points that help to integrate the scheme.

6

RUGS

Soft underfoot, rugs are a popular choice for bathrooms. Make sure that they are dried out after getting damp, to prevent them from rotting. They can be laid over wall-to-wall carpet, tiles, or wooden flooring. If laying them on slippery hard-tile floors, use a suitable nonslip backing.

CANDLES

Candles produce a wonderful relaxed feel in a bathroom, with scented varieties adding to this lovely calming atmosphere. However, always remember to use caution when dealing with naked flames. Make sure that the candles are not positioned too close to curtains or any flammable surfaces, and never leave them unattended.

6

INDEX

All illustrations by Chris Forsey. All photographs by Tim Ridley except for the following pages:

l = left, r = right, c = centre, t = top, b = bottom

Page 5b Arcaid; 7t Fritz von der Schulenberg/The Interior Archive; 8b Simon Kenny/Archaid; 12l Christopher Drake/Robert Harding Picture Library; 12r Nick Hofton/View; 13t Christopher Drake/Robert Harding Picture Library; 13b Camera Press; 30b Paul Ryan/International Interiors; 32t Paul Ryan/International Interiors; 32b Paul Ryan/International Interiors; 33 Trevor Mein/Arcaid; 41b Elizabeth Whiting & Associates; 56t Paul Ryan/International Interiors; 56b Elizabeth Whiting & Associates; 57t Elizabeth Whiting & Associates; 57b James Mortimer/The Interior Archive; 72t Elizabeth Whiting & Associates; 72b Elizabeth Whiting & Associates; 74tl Camera Press; 74tr Paul Ryan/International Interiors; 74b Fritz von der Schulenburg/The Interior Archive; 76l J.T.L Kurtz/Camera Press; 76r Elizabeth Whiting & Associates; 77tl Camera Press, 77tr Elizabeth Whiting & Associates; 77b Simon Kenny/Arcaid; 78t Elizabeth Whiting & Associates; 78b Peter Cook/View; 84t Elizabeth Whiting & Associates, 84bl Andrew Wood/The Interior Archive; 84b Camera Press; 89tl Arcaid; 89tr David Giles/Robert Harding Picture Library; 89b Peter Cook/View; 107c Elizabeth Whiting & Associates; 110t Elizabeth Whiting & Associates, 110b Fritz von der Schulenberg/Robert Harding Picture Library.